To Ed and May
Best of everything
John Kempfer

The Rogue Valley

by John Kemper

**Photographs by the Author
except where noted**

Outdoor Press
Medford, Oregon

OPPOSITE: Rogue Valley from Lower Table Rock

ACKNOWLEDGMENTS

I would like to express my deep appreciation to the people listed below, who helped me in finding and interpreting information about the wonderful Rogue Valley. Some of them reviewed sections of the manuscript, and thus helped me avoid mistakes. If any mistakes remain, they are solely my fault.

John Alexander, Klamath Bird Observatory
Jeffrey Alvis, Jacksonville Public Works Department
Margaret Bradford, Rogue Community College
Bruce Budamyr, Barnes and Noble
Frank Callahan, Crater Rock Museum
Chris and Stuart Freedman, Fire Mountain Gems and Beads
Terri Gieg, Jacksonville Chamber of Commerce
Ken Goddard, National Forensics Laboratory
Carol Harbison-Samuelson, Southern Oregon Historical Society
Daniel Hough, Jackson County Environmental Health Division
Stewart Janes, Southern Oregon University
Abby Jossie, Bureau of Land Management
Dana Parham, Grants Pass Tourism
Mary Pat Parker, Ashland Chamber of Commerce
Sarah Prewitt, Rogue Valley Manor
Roger Roberts, Jackson County Surveyor
Liz Shelby, Southern Oregon University
Larry Smith, Jacksonville Woodlands Association
Dennis Vroman, USDA Forest Service (retired)
Ted Warrick, Wooldridge Creek Vineyard
Julie Webster, Grants Pass Irrigation District

Contents

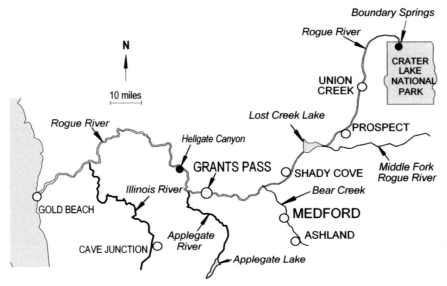

Figure 2 - The Rogue River and some of its major tributaries.

1 The Rogue Valley
"From Boundary Springs to Gold Beach"

When I first moved to the Rogue Valley, the thought occurred to me: *Just what do people mean, geographically, when they refer to the "Rogue Valley"?* It seemed to be an ordinary sort of question, but I got a surprising variety of interpretations.

One answer from a long-time resident of Ashland was, "It's everything from the source of the Rogue River near Crater Lake, to the ocean at Gold Beach." I liked that answer, and wanted to adopt it as my own, but I suspected that most Rogue Valley residents would have a different answer.

So, in my efforts to get a broad range of opinions, I asked a long-time Grants Pass resident my Rogue Valley question. She said, "It's the area around Grants Pass." I said, "But what about Medford?" Her answer: "No, Medford's not in the Rogue Valley." Perhaps what she had in mind is the fact that Grants Pass is directly on the Rogue River, but Medford is not. Medford is on Bear Creek.

So I asked another long-time resident of Grants Pass the same question. His answer was: "It's the valleys containing Medford and Grants Pass, extending to Ashland." When I asked him about the Applegate and Illinois Valleys, his answer was that they were not normally thought of as part of the Rogue Valley, but were their own valleys. I suspect this is the majority view.

Figure 1 - OPPOSITE PAGE - Rogue River at Tou Velle State Park

Then I came upon the definition as used by the wine industry. They define the boundaries of the "Rogue Valley American Viticultural Area" (also known as the "Rogue Valley Appellation") as including all four valleys -- Bear Creek Valley, the Applegate Valley, the Illinois Valley, and, of course, the valley of the Rogue River itself. To further complicate the matter, the Applegate Valley now has its own wine-country designation -- the Applegate Valley Appellation.

Finally, I sought an "official" answer. Nothing is more official on such matters than the Geographic Names Information System of the U.S. Geological Survey (USGS), on the Internet. When I put in the term "Rogue Valley, Oregon," I got back four entries -- all of them in Jackson County. They were: (1) Rogue Valley; (2) Valley of the Rogue State Park; (3) Rogue Valley Country Club; (4) Rogue Valley Memorial Hospital Heliport. I looked at the USGS topographic map for the first entry, and found the term "Rogue Valley" printed across the map in the region just north of Medford, between Central Point and the Table Rocks.

So, in the above, I've described five possible answers to my question, but I think the broad view of the majority is that the "Rogue Valley" extends roughly from Ashland to Grants Pass. It's obviously a subjective matter. But, whatever you choose as a definition, it's a marvelous region, as this book will attempt to show.

One of its marvels is its setting. The valley offers most of the advantages of major metropolitan areas, yet it is closely surrounded by beautiful mountains and forests that are only an hour or so away. These include such gems as Crater Lake, Mount Ashland, Howard Prairie, Hyatt Lake, and, of course, the incredible Rogue River, all easily reachable by paved highways. To residents, an accompanying miracle is that the traffic on the roads to these areas is usually quite light, when compared to the congestion near more heavily populated areas.

The State of Jefferson

In 1941, a group of citizens from Southern Oregon and Northern California proposed that a new state be organized, to be called "The State of Jefferson", because they felt they were not being treated fairly by California and Oregon. The new state would be composed of the counties of Siskiyou, Del Norte, and Modoc, in California, and Curry, Josephine, and Jackson, in Oregon. The capital would be the city of Yreka, in California. They even adopted a flag, showing a gold pan with two crosses on it, signifying the "double-cross" they felt they were getting from the two states.

Actually, the idea was not new. It had been proposed very early, in 1852, only two years after California became a state. A bill was introduced in the California State Legislature to create the "State of Shasta," but it went nowhere. The next year there was a similar proposal, to create what was to be called the "State of Klamath." It, too, went nowhere. The following year a proposal was advanced in the U.S. Congress to create what would be called either "Jackson Territory," or the "State of Jefferson." That, too, did not happen. Then the idea languished.

In 1941 the proposal was resurrected, and supporters even went so far as to set up road blocks on Highway 99, and hand out copies of the new state's "Proclamation of Independence" to motorists. Many people thought of it all as a prank, but in November, 1941, the residents of Yreka held an election for a provisional governor of the new state. There was a parade, an inauguration, and on December 6, 1941 the new officials met to get things moving.

On the very next day, the Japanese attacked Pearl Harbor, and the movement to create a new state collapsed. But then it was revived in the early 1990s, at least for California, when a proposal to divide California into two states was placed on the ballot. It lost.

However, a certain mystique had been created which exists to this day. Residents occasionally (and fondly) refer to themselves as living in the State of Jefferson, the public radio station on the campus of Southern Oregon University is called **Jefferson Public Radio,** a nature center in Medford is called **Jefferson Nature Center,** and there is a **State of Jefferson Scenic Byway** that runs down the Klamath River Canyon and up over the Siskiyous.

The Oregon-California Boundary

Here's a nice trivia question: Is the boundary between Oregon and California a straight line? Almost everyone would answer, "yes," and many would also know that the boundary lies along the 42nd parallel. Certainly, on the usual road maps we all use, the Oregon-California boundary is shown as a straight line.

But it is not straight, and wobbles back and forth quite a bit. Near Applegate Lake, in southern Jackson County, the deviation is about a half mile. The explanation is, back in the 1800s when the boundary was being surveyed, the intention was to place it precisely on the 42nd parallel. But, with the surveying instruments available at the time, deciding exactly where the 42nd parallel is, was no simple matter. So they made the survey, marking the border according to their data, and placed physical monuments on the ground. Not all of these, as it turned out, were precisely on the 42nd parallel. Once placed, and unless challenged in the courts, the monuments became the official boundary.

The Climate

The Rogue Valley has a terrific climate. It's as simple as that. The pattern is similar to that which generally prevails along the Pacific Coast -- rain concentrated in the months from October to April, with the summer months mostly free from rain. (Although Southern Oregonians are sometimes surprised by rain in the summer months.)

Oregon is supposed to be famous for its rain, and it does rain a lot along the coast and in the Willamette Valley. But the Rogue Valley is different. Someone once said to me, "The Rogue Valley is Oregon without the rain, and California without the people." I have never forgotten that.

Here are some numbers:

The **mean annual precipitation** in Medford is 18.8 inches. (This is about the same as Sacramento, California, which gets 17.4 inches.) Ashland is slightly greater. Grants Pass, which is 20 miles closer to the ocean than is Medford, gets more rain -- 30.8 inches. By contrast, Eugene, about 100 miles to the north, gets 45.9 inches. The sweepstakes winner for Oregon is a place in the Coast Range, which got 204.1 inches in 1996. Even that seems puny in comparison with the worlds' wettest spot, on Kauai, Hawaii, at 460 inches annually.

The **average maximum temperature** in Medford during July, the hottest month, is 90.5 degrees Fahrenheit. The average maximum for Ashland is a little less -- 86.9 degrees. The average maximum for Grants Pass is 89.9 degrees.

The **average minimum temperature** in Medford during January, the coldest month, is 30.4 degrees. In Ashland, it is 29.7 degrees, in Grants Pass, 32.5 degrees.

What about extremes? Chambers of Commerce like to stress averages, and prefer not to mention extremes. But extremes do occur, although not often. The hottest day in the last 70 years in Medford occurred in July 1946 -- 115 degrees. The coldest in the last 70 years occurred in December 1972 -- minus 6 degrees.

Snow does occur on the valley floor, but not often. Usually, it is an inch or two, perhaps a couple of times during the winter. Some winters may pass with none at all. But there have been some notable snow events in the past, such as in January 1930, when 22 inches of snow fell. But even Los Angeles occasionally gets snow, and I can recall the winter of 1949, when my wife and I were living in the Hollywood Hills, we got six inches of snow.

Crater Lake, at the head of the Rogue Valley, is famous for its snowfall. The average annual snowfall is 533 inches, and it is typical by early spring to have ten to fifteen feet of snow on the ground. The state record for snowfall belongs to Crater Lake, with 903 inches (75 feet) in 1950. The greatest depth of snow on the ground at one time, 21 feet, was recorded at Crater Lake Park Headquarters (elevation 6500 feet) in April, 1983.

Tornadoes have occurred in Oregon, but are mild compared to those in the Midwestern states. According to *The Oregon Weather Book,* they have occurred in the Willamette Valley and in the flatlands of eastern Oregon, but not in the Rogue Valley. The closest was a small one near Klamath Falls in May 1962 that destroyed a barn.

Whenever the matter of tornadoes comes up, the subject of **earthquakes** soon follows. The Pacific Coast states, of course, are known to be earthquake-prone. In the Pacific Northwest, the largest historic earthquake (magnitude 7.1) was in Olympia, Washington in 1949, which killed 8 people. The most destructive earthquake in Oregon (magnitude 5.6) in terms of property loss, occurred in 1993 southeast of Portland, which caused $30 million in damage. A monster earthquake (assumed magnitude of about 9), accompanied by a tsunami, apparently occurred off the Northwest coast in about 1700, destroying Native American villages along the coast. I found no records of significant earthquakes in the Rogue Valley, although a strong earthquake in Del Norte County, in California in 1873 caused some chimney damage in Jacksonville. A couple of earthquakes (magnitudes 5 and 6) occurred in the Klamath Falls area in 1993.

The **most notable storm** in Oregon's recorded history, according to *The Oregon Weather Book,* was the Columbus Day Storm of 1962. In most storms, the highest wind speeds are at coastal locations, but in 1962 a wind speed of 116 miles per hour (mph) was recorded in Portland. *The Oregon Weather Book* doesn't say how strong the winds were in the Rogue Valley in the Columbus Day Storm, but in November 1981, a wind speed of 62 mph was recorded in Medford, and in March 1987, 70 mph was recorded in Ashland.

But extremes are, well, extreme, and no place, however idyllic, is immune to them. It is no exaggeration to say that the climate in the Rogue Valley is among the finest anywhere, and the sign arching over the main street of Grants Pass says it very well indeed: "It's the Climate."

The Quality of the Air

The question of air pollution in the Rogue Valley sometimes arises. The valley is a basin, surrounded by mountains, that often has calm days in winter. The conditions are perfect for what is known as a "temperature inversion," which causes the air temperature close to the ground to be lower than it is higher. The result is that the air close to the ground, along with any pollutants it contains, tends to be trapped there. Another result is that the valley often has fog in the winter. The fog can often be escaped by gaining a few hundred feet in elevation, by going up into the hills.

Some key elements in monitoring air quality are **fine particulate matter, carbon monoxide**, and **ozone**. Industry at one time was the principal source of air pollution in the valley, but because of measures which have been taken to control pollution from industry, motor vehicles have now become a major source of pollution, especially for ozone. The Medford area (including Ashland and Eagle Point) is one region (Portland is the other) that requires vehicles to pass a "clean air test." As a result, carbon monoxide levels in the valley have come down significantly from what they were in the 1980s, and ozone has remained relatively constant, in spite of the increasing number of automobiles.

In the past, fine particulate matter was a special air quality problem for the Rogue Valley, mostly because of wood stoves and outdoor burning. The "energy crisis" of the 1970s brought a major increase in the number of wood-burning stoves, which caused increases of airborne particulate matter in the valley. As a consequence, ordinances were adopted that required the use of "clean-burning" stoves, and also established controls for outdoor burning. The graph in Figure 3 shows the 20-year trend in Medford for what is called PM_{10}, and shows a marked improvement in particulate matter of that size. (The term "PM_{10}" refers to fine particulates less than 10 microns* in diameter.) However, the emphasis is shifting away from particles of 10 microns to those which are 2.5 microns or less in diameter, because it is believed the smaller particles are critical.

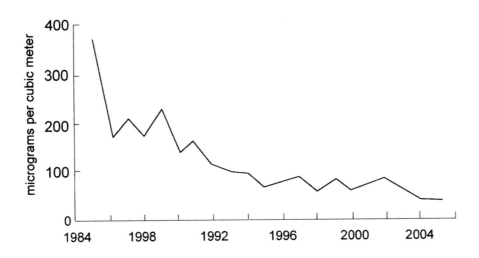

Figure 3 - Fine particulate matter (PM_{10}) in Medford, using 2nd highest 24 hr average

A major set of events that Rogue Valley residents will long remember were the forest fires of 2002, which burned almost 500,000 acres of forest land west of the Illinois Valley

---

*A micron is one-millionth of a meter. Human hair ranges from 50 to 150 microns in diameter.

(known as the "Biscuit Fire"), and 88,000 acres to the north of Jackson County (known as the "Tiller Fire"). Smoke from the fires reached the Rogue Valley and stayed for long periods of time. However, events like wildfires don't "count" in air pollution records, because the regulations are concerned with human-caused events. Nevertheless, smoke from wildfires can cause just as much distress to individuals as from human-caused fires.

The Population

Some quick facts, regarding approximate populations as of 2004:
Jackson County: 193,000
Josephine County: 80,000
Medford: 68,000
Grants Pass: 21,000
Ashland: 20,400

Jackson County had an annual growth rate of 1½% in the early 2000s. This doesn't seem like much, but, if continued, would produce 30,000 more people in Jackson County by 2014.

A result of population growth, of course, is an escalation in housing prices. According to the Southern Oregon Workforce Housing Summit, in Ashland the average resale price of a home went from $250,000 in 2000, to $460,000 in 2005. In Medford, the average resale price in 2005 was $305,000, and in Grants Pass it was $250,000. In certain locations in the Jackson/Josephine counties area, there were homes in the $1,000,000 to $2,000,000 range, and some were even higher.

The Economy

It's no secret that the economy of Southern Oregon once was heavily dependent upon the timber harvest. It's also no secret that the timber harvest has gone into a severe decline, partly because of pressures from environmentalists who are opposed to logging, including litigation, and partly because of economic competition from other countries. The production in thousands of board feet (MBF) of timber for Jackson and Josephine counties combined was 1,002,000 MBF in 1955, and 159,000 MBF in 2004, a decline of almost 85%. In 2004, two-thirds of the total came from private lands, whereas in prior years most of it had come from public lands.

In the 50 years or so during which timber harvest declined, the economy of the Rogue Valley changed radically. The valley has long been noted for its pears, of course, although the acreage devoted to pears declined from its peak of 12,000 acres, to about 8000 in 1985. Pears and other fruits are still important, and the wine industry has been increasing in importance, but other aspects of the overall economy have become even more prominent.

The Oregon Employment Department said, in 2005: ". . . the economy of today [of Jackson and Josephine counties] represents a diverse mix of industries that provides goods and services . . . The area is increasingly becoming a retail and services hub that serves a population much larger than the 260,000 residents of the two-county region." The Employment Department said that other important industries include "art, entertainment and recreation, health care and social assistance, accommodations, and food services," and added, "A steady stream of near- and retirement-age residents from other locations also has benefited the Rogue Valley's health services and residential care facilities industries. . . . The region is expected to add jobs faster than any region of the state."

6

The cost of electricity is an important component of any economy, and Oregon is one of the states with low cost, at an average cost to residential customers of 7.42 cents per kilowatt-hour (kwh) in 2006. Customers in Washington paid less -- 6.68 cents per kwh, while customers in California paid more -- 13.4 cents per kwh. Massachusetts was the highest-cost state in the continental U.S., at 17.64 cents per kwh. More than 80% of Oregon's electricity in 2006 came from coal and natural gas, with 13% from hydropower, and 2% from wind.

In 2005, the seven largest employers in the two counties were (number of employees shown in parentheses):

Asante Health System (3,782)
(Includes Rogue Valley Medical Center in Medford, and Three Rivers
Community Hospital in Grants Pass, plus others)
Harry and David Operations (3,500)
(Includes headquarters, packing houses and orchards, and Jackson and
Perkins roses.)
Providence Medical Center (1,150)
Medford School District (1,083)
Jackson County (1,023)
Boise Building Solutions (970)
(Formerly, Boise Cascade. Plywood and engineered wood products.)
Southern Oregon University (822)

Harry and David is one of the most highly visible organizations in the Rogue Valley, and one of the best known. At the peak of the holiday season, its normal work force may temporarily swell to over 6,700 employees. The company began when Samuel Rosenberg, a successful hotel owner in Seattle, bought 240 acres of pears in the Rogue Valley and named them Bear Creek Orchards. In 1914, Samuel Rosenberg died, and his two sons, Harry and David, took over. In the depression years of the 1930s, Harry and David searched for new markets for their pears, and came up with the idea of a mail order business, which turned out to be enormously successful. In 1966, they purchased **Jackson and Perkins,** a major wholesale rose producer, and incorporated it into their mail order operations. Reservations for tours can be made through **Harry and David's Country Village**, on Center Drive near Stewart Avenue in South Medford.

Rogue Valley Manor is also highly visible, because of its two big buildings that are perched on a hill on the southeastern side of Medford, near the I-5 freeway. The two buildings offer apartment living for retirees, but there are also about 300 cottages surrounding the two buildings, each with 1, 2, or 3 bedrooms. There are also two golf courses, one 9-hole (Quail Point Golf Course), and the other an 18-hole championship course (Centennial Golf Club). Rogue Valley Manor is a part of Pacific Retirement Services (PRS), which oversees about a dozen retirement communities in Oregon, Washington, California, and Texas. In addition, PRS operates 24 affordable housing communities.

"The Dom", on Highway 62 north of Medford, is another prominent element of the Rogue Valley scene. Prior to 2004, it was known as the White City Domiciliary (hence, "The Dom"), belonging to the U.S. Veterans Health Administration. In 2004 it was re-named the **Southern Oregon Rehabilitation Center and Clinics,** but retained all the services it had prior to the re-naming, offering ". . .quality residential treatment in psychiatry, addictions, medicine, bio-psychosocial, physical, and vocational rehabilitation." In spite of the name change, many long-time residents still refer to it as "The Dom."

Rogue Valley International Medford Airport

Daily non-stop flights are available from Medford to Seattle, Portland, San Francisco, Los Angeles, and Phoenix. The airport in 2005 served nearly 600,000 passengers. The only other airports in Southern Oregon with scheduled flights are in Klamath Falls and North Bend. Jackson County has airports for private planes at Ashland, Prospect, and Shady Cove. Josephine County has airports for private planes at Grants Pass and the Illinois Valley.

Many people ask a question about the word "International" in the name of the Medford airport. Where are the international flights? The word occurs because in 1995 the airport was awarded a "foreign trade zone" designation, and was authorized as an international port of entry by the U.S. Customs Service, Immigration and Naturalization Agency. Its intended purpose is to handle cargo, rather than passengers. The zone has become inactive, but the authorization is maintained, in anticipation of reactivating.

Figure 4 - Vineyard in Applegate Valley
(Courtesy of Wooldridge Creek Vineyard)

The Wine Industry

The Wine Industry has been in Southern Oregon for a long time, and is increasing in importance. As described earlier, there are three wine-growing regions included in the Rogue Valley American Viticultural Area, often just called the "Rogue Valley Appellation."

The **Bear Creek Valley**, from Ashland to Medford, has eight wineries, almost all of which offer tasting to the public. There is also a winery in Shady Cove, which is not in Bear Creek Valley, but is within the area of the Rogue Valley Appellation. Bear Creek Valley is the driest and warmest of the three valleys. Its climate is considered similar to that of France's Bordeaux region. Grape varieties that are grown include cabernet sauvignon, merlot, chardonnay, cabernet franc, pinot gris, sauvignon blanc, malbec, and syrah.

The **Applegate Valley** now has its own appellation, but is still regarded as part of the Rogue Valley Appellation. It is intermediate in dryness and warmth between the Bear Creek Valley and the valley to the west, the Illinois Valley. It has 12 wineries, most of which offer tasting to the public. The wineries have organized themselves into what they call the **Applegate Valley Wine Trail.** Grapes that are grown include chardonnay, merlot, cabernet sauvignon, pinot noir, cabernet franc, viognier, sangiovese, syrah, malbec, petit verdot, tempranillo, and zinfandel.

The **Illinois Valley** is a little higher in elevation than the others, and subject to more marine influences. It has three wineries, and all of them offer public tasting. Grapes that are grown are those that are usually associated with France's Burgundy region, and include pinot noir, gewurztraminer, riesling, pinot gris, chardonnay, pinot blanc, early muscat, and gamay noir.

Mount McLoughlin? Or Mount Pitt?

The dominant feature of the Rogue Valley is unquestionably Mount McLoughlin (cover photo, and Figure 5), which rises at the eastern border of Jackson County. But there is a difficulty with the name: many old-timers don't call it Mount McLoughlin, but call it Mount Pitt. (Or sometimes, Mount Pit; the spellings vary.) What's going on here?

The earliest printed reference to the area is on a map published in 1838, in a book by Reverend Samuel Parker, called *Journal of an Exploring Tour Beyond the Rocky Mountains, in 1835, '36, and '37.* The Reverend Parker apparently did not personally see the mountain, but he clearly shows the name "Mount McLaughlin" on his map. The trouble is that the mountain thus named lies at the head of the "Umbiqua River" [Umpqua River], about in the position of Mount Thielsen. A little further south on the map, but well north of what is shown as "Clamet River" [Klamath River], is a mountain labeled "Mt. Shasty." Again, there is some trouble with this: the mountain we now know as Mount Shasta is *south* of the Klamath River, not north of it. The mountain that the Reverend Parker labeled as "Mt. Shasty," is shown about where the present Mount McLoughlin is located.

Well, the Reverend Parker apparently was working from information transmitted to him from others, possibly from Peter Skene Ogden or his associates. (See Chapter 3.) Other geographical features on the reverend's map are shown rather accurately, such as Fort Vancouver, Mount St. Helens, and Mount Hood. However, even though Mount McLoughlin is located in the wrong place on the map, this represents the earliest use of the name (although the Reverend Parker spelled it "Mount McLaughlin").

The name "Mount Pitt" first appeared on a map made in 1843, stemming from John Charles Fremont's 1843 expedition. The presumption is that the name "Pitt" was a reference to the pits dug by Indians of the region to trap game. The name was sometimes spelled "Pit" and sometimes "Pitt." The river known today as "Pit River" flows through the region south and east of Mount Shasta.

Indians called the mountain *M'Laiksini Yaina,* meaning "steep mountain." Early settlers in the Rogue Valley called it "Snowy Butte," or "Big Butte." At least one attempt was made to call it "Mount Adams," but this failed. During the Civil War, the name "Mount Pitt" came into wide use.

In 1905, the Oregon legislature officially adopted the name "Mount McLoughlin," and this name in turn was adopted by the United States Board of Geographic Names. The name honored Dr. John McLoughlin, who was the chief factor of the Hudson's Bay Company at Fort Vancouver. During his time as chief factor, he welcomed Americans, even though sovereignty over the area was in dispute between the United States and England. In 1849, Dr. McLoughlin moved from Fort Vancouver to Oregon City, and became an American citizen.

The mountain is climbable, but it is arduous, suitable only for people in good condition. It is an 11-mile round trip, and there is an elevation gain of 4000 feet to the summit at 9,495 feet. The route is over rocky terrain, and in places is difficult to follow. Much of it is above timberline. The Forest Service warns that people often lose their way on the mountain, especially while coming down.

Since Mount McLoughlin is a volcano, a natural question is, "Is it likely to erupt?" The answer appears to be "no," but the U.S. Geological Survey (USGS) carefully avoids stating whether any particular volcano is extinct. However, in the case of Mount McLoughlin, the USGS says the last eruptions apparently were about 20,000 to 30,000 years ago, and possibly more.

There are volcanoes in the Cascade Range that are indeed active, as the 1980 eruption of Mount St. Helens in Washington shows. Prior to the St. Helens eruption, Mount Lassen, in California, erupted in 1914. Mount Hood, near Portland, Mount Rainier, in Washington, and Mount Shasta, in California, all had eruptions in the 1700s and 1800s. Mount Mazama, which contains the incomparably beautiful Crater Lake, erupted about 8000 years ago. Interestingly, the largest Cascade volcano of all (in total volume, not height) is hardly perceived by most people as being a volcano at all. It is **Medicine Lake Volcano**, just south of the Oregon-California line. From a distance, it looks like an ordinary range of mountains. Inside the caldera, the forests slope down to a lake in the middle, called Medicine Lake. The lake has campgrounds, and is popular for fishing. The surroundings don't look anything at all like a proper volcano. But it last erupted about 900 years ago, and **Lava Beds National Monument** in California is on the northern slope of the mountain.

The Bigfoot Trap

No account of the Rogue Valley would be complete without mentioning **Bigfoot,** the elusive, hairy, 7-foot dweller of the forests. In Canada, they call it "Sasquatch," and in Asia, "Yeti," or the "Abominable Snowman." Sightings have been reported in all parts of North America, but the majority of them are concentrated in the Pacific Northwest, mostly in Washington and British Columbia, but many of them in Oregon. Other than the sightings, there are photographs and plaster casts of footprints, and there is even a home movie of a

Figure 5 - Mount McLoughlin from Howard Prairie

Bigfoot walking along a creekbed, taken in California. (Skeptics claim it was just a man in a gorilla suit.) After decades of sightings, no physical evidence in the form of a specimen, or of bones, has turned up. Nevertheless, there are many Bigfoot believers. And also, many Bigfoot skeptics.

In the early 1970s, a group from Eugene, Oregon received a permit from the National Forest Service to construct a Bigfoot trap in the Rogue River National Forest, near Applegate Lake. The trap was 10 feet by 10 feet, and was constructed of heavy timbers, reinforced with steel plates and bolts. It reportedly was baited with something "real stinky." The plan was, if a Bigfoot entered the trap to get the bait, things were rigged so the door would slam down.

They never caught a Bigfoot, although some think they may have caught a bear once. After a few years, the group gave up, and let their permit lapse. The trap is still there, although the Forest Service has welded the door in the "open" position, so no one will get caught. Its location is even marked on the Forest Service map. To get there: from Medford take Highway 238 to Ruch, and turn toward Applegate Lake. A short distance beyond the Applegate Lake dam, there is a pull-off at the Collings Mountain Trailhead, on the right, where you can park. The Bigfoot Trap is about ½ mile along the trail. Watch out for poison oak.

Figure 7 - Ospreys are seen frequently along the Rogue River. Their bulky nests are conspicuous, usually placed in the tops of dead trees, or on power poles. The power company often will construct a nesting platform for the birds, above the wires, so they won't get electrocuted.

2 The River

"Stream of Life"

The Rogue River was given the name of "stream of life" by a Grants Pass newspaper. Clearly, the name is appropriate, because the river is the vital thread that holds the region together.

At 215 miles long, it is one of the bigger rivers in the state. The Columbia River is much larger, but Oregon has to share the Columbia with other states. Of those rivers lying wholly within Oregon, the ranking is as shown on the next page. (Average annual discharge is shown in acre-feet. An acre-foot is the amount of water one acre in extent and one foot deep.)

Figure 6 - OPPOSITE PAGE - Wild and Scenic Rogue River, below Grave Creek.

Willamette River (27,500,000 acre-feet)
Umpqua River (6,700,000 acre-feet)
Rogue River (5,700,000 acre-feet)
Deschutes River (4,200,000 acre-feet)

The Illinois River is the largest tributary of the Rogue, with an average annual discharge rate of almost 3,000,000 acre-feet. By comparison, the Klamath, another large river, has an average annual discharge rate of 1,400,000 acre-feet at the point where it leaves Oregon and enters California,.

Beginnings

All rivers begin with springs, but not many rivers begin with springs as big as those of the Rogue River. The volcanic mountains of the Cascades act somewhat like a gigantic sponge, absorbing the snow melt into porous soil, and then, in places, releasing the water as big springs. In some notable cases, the rivers come out at full force from dry rocky surroundings, forming an "instant river."

The best known such river in the state is the **Metolius River** near the town of Sisters in Central Oregon. The U.S. Forest Service has provided an improved access area there, with a paved foot trail. Another is the **Wood River,** one of the major tributaries of the Klamath River. The source of Wood River is easily viewed at Kimball State Park, near Fort Klamath, north of Klamath Falls.

In the case of the Rogue, there are several large spring systems at the headwaters. The best known is **Boundary Springs**, which is recognized as the "official" source of the Rogue River. The springs are on the slopes of Mount Mazama, the mountain that contains Crater Lake, and get their name from the fact that they lie close to the boundary of Crater Lake National Park. They are accessible by a 5-mile hike (round trip). The starting point is at the Crater Rim Viewpoint parking area on OR 230, about 18.5 miles north of the intersection of OR 230 and OR 62 (see map in Figure 8).

Another is **Thousand Springs**. To get there, from the junction of OR 230 and OR 62 go about 5.7 miles on OR 62 to a gravel road on the right, just beyond the Thousand Springs Sno-Park. Turn on the gravel road, and, at the first intersection take the left-hand road. It is about two miles to Thousand Springs, which are marked. The springs lie just inside the boundary of Crater Lake National Park (see Figure 8).

And then there are **Big Butte Springs.** The springs lie at the foot of Mount McLoughlin, about six miles east of the town of Butte Falls, along the Butte Falls-Fish Lake Road. There is no public access, since it is Medford's municipal water supply. Up until the 1950s, virtually all of Medford's water came from the springs. From its origin, the water travels some 30 miles in a double underground pipeline to Medford. In the 1950s, it was decided that this source needed to be augmented by water taken directly from the Rogue River, and the Duff Water Treatment Plant was constructed near Tou Velle State Park. During the time when all of Medford's water came from Big Butte Springs, the slogan of the Medford Water Commission was "A mountain spring in every home."

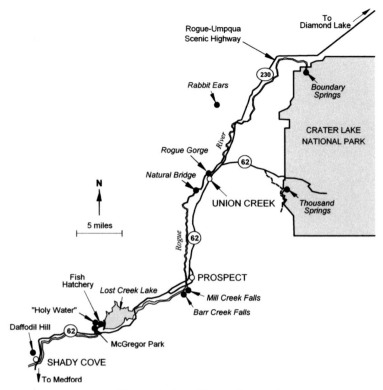

Figure 8 - The Upper Rogue River

Redirecting the flows

An intriguing aspect of the Rogue River is that some of its flow actually comes from the opposite side of the Cascade divide -- water that in former times flowed into the Klamath River.

A part of the water comes from **Fourmile Lake,** which is on the eastern side of the Cascade Divide near Lake of the Woods. In 1923, a canal and tunnel were constructed, leading from Fourmile Lake back under the divide and into Fish Lake, adjacent to OR 140. From Fish Lake, the water flows into Little Butte Creek, and then into the system of the Medford Irrigation District. Ultimately, of course, it finds its way into the Rogue.

Further south, at **Howard Prairie Lake** and **Hyatt Lake** (both of which were created by dams), the natural drainage again would have taken the water into the Klamath River. But the outflows of each are captured in Keene Creek Reservoir. (OR 66 loops around Keene Creek Reservoir, just after it crosses the Cascade Divide at Green Springs Summit. See map on Page 51.) The water coming from Hyatt Lake flows directly into Keene Creek Reservoir, but the water from Howard Prairie Lake arrives via a long canal.

From Keene Creek Reservoir, the water is sent through a tunnel under the divide at Green Springs Summit. It generates some electrical power at the Green Springs Powerplant (16,000 kilowatts), and then goes into Emigrant Lake near Ashland. From Emigrant Lake, the water

15

flows into Bear Creek, and finally, into the Rogue. A major part of it is used for irrigation, delivered through the canals of Talent Irrigation District. (See Page 82, about the Talent Irrigation District.)

Upper Rogue

The part of the river that is generally thought of as the "Upper Rogue" runs from Boundary Springs to Shady Cove. (See map, Figure 8.) From its source to Prospect, it has been designated as a "Wild and Scenic River," and it is paralleled by the **Rogue-Umpqua Scenic Byway**. The scenic byway begins in Roseburg and ends in Gold Hill, running near both the North Umpqua River and the Rogue River along the way.

Much of the highway from the Boundary Springs area to Union Creek passes through a beautiful forest of large trees. Several times, the road comes close to the river, which here flows smoothly through grassy banks and lush forest. About 5 miles north of the junction of OR 230 and OR 62 there are stunning views of **Rabbit Ears**, a remarkable remnant of an old volcano.

Union Creek

The "center" of the Upper Rogue is **Union Creek,** which has operated as a stopping place along the road since it was first constructed as a military road in the late 19th century, running from Jacksonville to Fort Klamath. The "village" of Union Creek consists of the **Union Creek Resort** and **Beckie's Cafe.** The resort, with cabins and a country store, is listed on the National Register of Historic Places, and has been in operation since the early 1900s. It is claimed that Zane Grey, Jack London, and Herbert Hoover all were visitors there. Beckie's Cafe is named for Ed Beckelhymer, who built a garage and delicatessen at Union Creek in 1921.

Nearby is **Rogue Gorge Viewpoint**, with a delightful paved trail about ¼ mile long, barrier-free, that leads along the edge of the gorge. There are observation platforms, and one of them literally overhangs the lip of the gorge. At this point, the gorge is deeper (45 feet) than it is wide (25 feet from the edge of the platform to the opposite rim). Below, the water surges in a white torrent between the narrow walls. It is said that the gorge was created by the

Figure 9 - Beckie's Cafe at Union Creek

collapse of an old lava tube, and there are actually a couple of collapsed tubes visible on the opposite side.

A short distance down the road from Union Creek is **Natural Bridge,** where there is a paved barrier-free trail about 0.3 mile long that leads to the river and along it. Several viewing platforms give vantage points to see the river as it enters an old lava tube and then surges forth again downstream, creating the natural "bridge."

From Union Creek to Prospect, the road does not run near the river, but passes through a magnificent forest. In spring, the forest glows with the white flowers of the Pacific dogwood. In October, the leaves of the dogwood turn a delicate rosy color. Also, in fall, the vine maples turn red in the sun and yellow in the shade. As you drive through the forest, the leaves appear to have an internal glow, lighting up the woods.

The entire stretch of the river from Boundary Springs to Prospect is paralleled by the **Upper Rogue River Trail**. The trail can be hiked in segments, since it is crossed by gravel roads in many places.

Figure 10 - Rogue Gorge

Prospect

The village of **Prospect** contains the **Prospect Hotel,** which is listed on the National Register of Historic Places. The hotel dates from the 1880s, and claims an even longer list of celebrities than does the Union Creek Resort, including not only Zane Grey, Jack London, and Herbert Hoover, but also William Jennings Bryan, John Muir, Gifford Pinchot, and Theodore Roosevelt.

Figure 11 - Mill Creek Falls

At Prospect, a side road goes to a parking area for two fine waterfalls, **Mill Creek Falls** (173 feet high), and **Barr Creek Falls** (200 feet high). A trail leads to them, about 0.3 mile to Mill Creek Falls, and 0.1 mile further to Barr Creek Falls. There are good viewpoints for both, but neither viewpoint is protected by a fenced barrier, making them risky for children.

Between Prospect and Lost Creek Lake there is a power plant on the Rogue, fed from a holding pond on the river near Prospect. At one point, the highway passes over the huge penstocks feeding the plant, which produces 36,000 kilowatts of electric energy.

Lost Creek Lake

A major feature of the Rogue below Prospect is **Lost Creek Lake**. This is a large reservoir, about 10 miles long, with a dam 327 feet high. An interesting feature of the lake is that there are actually <u>two</u> creeks named "Lost Creek," one entering the lake on the north side, and one on the south.

The primary purpose of the dam is flood control, with power generation, water supply, and recreation as additional purposes. **Joseph H. Stewart State Recreation Area,** with a campground, picnic area, and marina is on the south shore of the lake adjacent to the highway. A trail system, bearing the name "Rogue River Trail" runs on both sides of the lake. (Note that the name "Rogue River Trail" is also applied to a trail through the roadless part of the Lower Rogue River canyon. See page 23.) Much of the trail through Stewart Park is paved, for bicycle travel.

The dam which creates Lost Creek Lake is called **William L. Jess Dam.** The power plant associated with the dam generates about 50,000 kilowatts. This dam is one of three that were authorized in 1962, under what was called the "Rogue River Basin Project." The dam at Lost

Figure 12 - Autumn leaves along the Upper Rogue

Creek was completed by the Corps of Engineers in 1977, and the second one, the Applegate Dam, was completed in 1980. The third, called "Elk Creek Dam" was partially built, but never completed because of environmental lawsuits. (Elk Creek is about 5 miles downstream from Lost Creek Lake.) Since the partially-completed dam makes it impossible for fish to migrate upstream, the Corps of Engineers adopted a program of capturing adult fish below the dam, and carrying them by truck around the dam to the upstream waters.

Between the dam at Lost Creek Lake and the fish hatchery a short distance downstream is a quiet stretch of water known to fishermen as the **"Holy Water,"** because of the huge fish that have been caught there. The Holy Water is open to fly-fishing only, "catch-and-release." **Rivers Edge Park** lies on both sides of the river at the Holy Water, which is of interest not only because of its fishing, but also because of the large concentrations of waterfowl, of many species, that collect here in the winter.

The **Cole M. Rivers Hatchery**, the largest in Oregon, lies just downstream from the Holy Water. Because of the dam at the hatchery, this is as far as the fish can go when they come upriver to spawn. Adult salmon and steelhead are captured, their eggs are collected, and the young fish are hatched and raised at the hatchery. Since the adult salmon will die anyway after spawning, they are killed before being stripped of eggs and sperm. Steelhead, on the other hand, may spawn naturally more than once, so the hatchery releases adult steelhead back into the river.

Most of the young fish raised at the hatchery are put back into the Rogue, but many are distributed to other streams and lakes in the Rogue Basin. About 3.5 million fish are raised annually at the hatchery. Nearly 2 million of these are chinook salmon, 300,000 are coho salmon, 600,000 are steelhead, and 800,000 are rainbow trout.

Just downstream from the hatchery is **McGregor Park**, operated by the Corps of Engineers. It is a delightful place for a picnic or a stroll on the trail by the river.

From Lost Creek Lake to Shady Cove, the highway runs close to the river. This section of the river is popular for fishing, boating, and rafting, although it is lined in many places with homes and ranches. The community of **Trail** is just north of Shady Cove, and was named because an Indian trail came over the divide at this point, leading from the Umpqua River to the Rogue River.

Shady Cove is a small community with a population of about 2,500, that calls itself "The Jewel of the Upper Rogue." It sponsors numerous events. One of them is **"Daffodil Daze"** in March, when the daffodils (claimed to be over a million plants) at nearby **Daffodil Hill** bloom. Others are an annual wildflower show (May), salmon barbecue (July), a "river art walk" (August), and a quilt show (November). An unusual event is the **Spam Parade and BBQ,** a just-for-fun event celebrating the well-known canned meat.

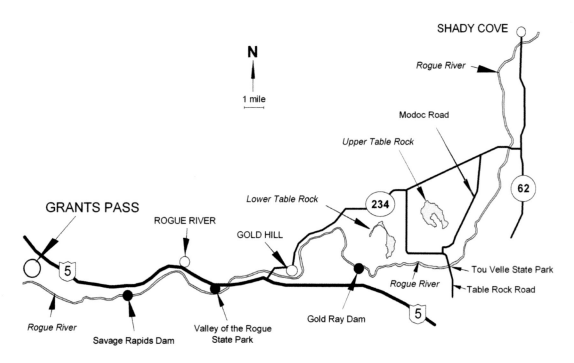

Figure 13 - Middle Rogue River

Middle Rogue

From Shady Cove to Tou Velle State Park, the river generally is not visible from the main roads, with the exception of one road crossing at Highway 234. There are some large homes and ranches in this section. **Ginger Rogers,** of the famed Ginger Rogers-Fred Astaire movie dance team, purchased a 1000-acre ranch along the river here in 1940. She lived on the ranch with her mother for the next 50 years., when not starring in movies. (See Page 79.)

Tou Velle State Park

Tou Velle State Park is about 14 miles downstream from Shady Cove, and is a delightful day-use park directly on the river. To get there from Medford, go north on OR 62 5.8 miles to Antelope Road, and turn west. Go 1.8 miles on Antelope Road to Table Rock Road and turn right (north). The park lies 0.8 mile north, just before the bridge on the Rogue River. Directly across the bridge, on the opposite side of Table Rock Road, is another section of the park, with a boat launch facility.

Incidentally, there are at least three variations of the way to spell the name of the park: Tou Velle, TouVelle, and Touvelle, that are seen on road signs and maps. The person for whom the park is named apparently spelled his name Frank TouVelle. He was an orchardist, and served as a judge in Jackson County.

In the fall, when salmon come up the river to spawn, the riffles alongside the exposed gravel bars in the middle of the river are attractive to the fish for spawning. Also, great blue herons in the early spring congregate for nesting purposes. Directly across the river from the entrance kiosk is a grove of tall cottonwood trees containing a rookery of a dozen or so great blue heron nests, high in the trees.

A short nature trail begins at the far eastern end of the parking lot. It goes along the edge of the river and then loops back, about ½ mile round trip. If you continue along the river instead of taking the loop trail, you soon come to the **Ken Denman Wildlife Area**, and a gravel road. The road is from the time when all of this area was a part of **Camp White,** a major army installation during World War II. (See Chapter 9, "Medford.") After the war, much of Camp White was given to the state as a wildlife area.

North of Tou Velle State Park are the famous **Table Rocks.** (See Page 48.)

Gold Hill, Rogue River, and the Oregon Vortex

The Rogue soon enters a narrow canyon, where it is joined by the railroad tracks of the Central Oregon and Pacific Railroad. Near the point where the railroad joins the river is **Gold Ray Dam.** (See Figure 14, next page.) The dam was constructed in 1902 by Frank H. and C.R. Ray. In 1907 they named their company the **Rogue River Electric Company,** and began supplying power to several valley communities. By 1972, when the power plant was decommissioned, it had been generating 1,250 kilowatts. The dam subsequently passed into the ownership of Jackson County, and at this writing is inactive, with an indefinite future. The dam is equipped with fish ladders and a fish counting station, where a regular count is made by the Oregon Fish and Wildlife Department, of the numbers of chinook, coho, and steelhead ascending the river.

There is another old dam between Gold Ray Dam and Gold Hill, called the **Gold Hill Diversion Dam.** Its purpose was to divert water into a canal as a water supply for the city of

Figure 14 - Gold Ray Dam and Lower Table Rock

Gold Hill. As of 2006, a new water supply system had been installed by the city at a cost of $1.2 million, and the dam was slated for removal, at a cost of another $1.8 million.

Downstream from **Gold Hill,** the river is paralleled by I-5 as far as Grants Pass. Gold Hill is a small community of about 1000 people. Nearby is the **Oregon Vortex,** open from March until October. To get to the vortex, go 1.5 miles west from Gold Hill on Highway 234 to Sardine Creek Road, turn right, and go 4.2 miles. (Admission charge.) The owners of the vortex say there is a "spherical field of force" here, which causes visitors to experience various paranormal effects, with objects seeming to roll uphill, or balance at odd angles.

Between Gold Hill and the City of Rogue River is **Valley of the Rogue State Park.** This delightful park has a picnic area, a large campground, and a one-mile **River's Edge Interpretive Trail.**

Next is the town of **Rogue River,** with about 2000 inhabitants. Each year, in June, the city hosts a three-day **Rooster Crow Weekend**, which features a parade, a car show, a quilt show, a 5K run, and the "National Rooster Crow Championship." The rooster that crows the most during a 30-minute period is the champion. The contest has been going since 1953, and the all-time winner was a rooster named "White Lightning," who crowed 112 times in 30 minutes.

Savage Rapids Dam

And then we have the **Savage Rapids Dam,** about halfway between the city of Rogue River and Grants Pass. The dam is 39 feet high, and was originally constructed in 1921. Its purpose was to provide irrigation water to the Grants Pass Irrigation District. On one side of the dam, the water flows by gravity into a system of canals. On the other, the water must be pumped, to enter the system. The pumps are not electrical, but are hydraulically driven turbines, with the pressure supplied by the height of the dam.

The big issue has been the passage of fish. There are two fish ladders, one on each side of the dam, and adult salmon mostly manage to negotiate these ladders and proceed on upstream. But there is a problem for the small fish coming downstream in the spring, heading to the ocean. The pump turbines create a strong suction, and many small fish are pulled into the turbines and die.

In 2001, after years of costly legal battles, the Grants Pass Irrigation District signed a federal consent decree for the removal of the dam, and the installation of electrically driven pumps (with fish screens) to supply irrigation water. It was anticipated that most of the money to take down the dam and install the pumps, estimated at $30 million, would come from the Federal Government.

The Rogue River passes directly through the center of Grants Pass. Grants Pass, as a major city in the Rogue Valley, has a special chapter, Chapter 10.

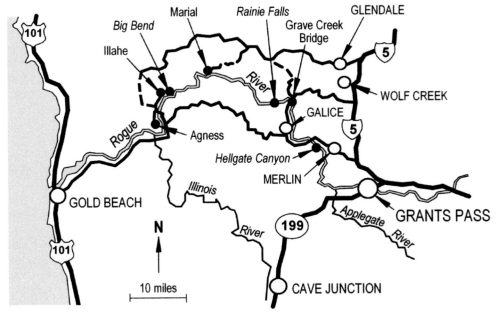

Figure 15 - Lower Rogue River

Lower Rogue

The Lower Rogue is the most famous part of the river, hands-down. Jet boats, departing from Grants Pass, carry tourists through **Hellgate Canyon,** a narrow canyon gorge about 15 miles downstream. Hellgate has been the scene of numerous movies, including "Rooster Cogburn" (with John Wayne and Katherine Hepburn) and "The River Wild" (with Meryl Streep).

From Hellgate to Grave Creek, a distance of about 15 miles, the Merlin-Galice Road parallels the river closely. Much of this section is popular with rafters, but it is at Grave Creek where the real action begins. From Grave Creek almost to the coast, the Rogue has been designated as a Wild and Scenic River. The paved road along the river ends at Grave Creek, and from this point until **Foster Bar,** near Agness, a distance of 34 river miles, there is no road, although a gravel road reaching down from the north touches the river at Marial. This section of the canyon has the part of the **Rogue River Trail** that is best known.

Numerous rafting companies offer 3- and 4-day trips down the wild Rogue, with some of the trips spending the nights at lodges on the river, and others offering campouts. You can also hike the Rogue River Trail along the river, on your own if you want to, or as a participant in commercial trips of various sorts, generally 4 or 5 days long. On the commercial trips, you can either stay at a lodge each night along the way, or camp, with your camping equipment carried to you each day by a raft.

The Rogue River Trail begins at the **Grave Creek Bridge** (see map, Figure 15) and follows the river, along the north side of the canyon. At the opposite end of the Grave Creek Bridge there is a trailhead and roadside parking for the trail to **Rainie Falls,** about 2 miles long. The trail is considered easy by most persons, although there are several ups and downs, some of them steep. In places, the trail consists of narrow rocky ledges that have literally been hacked out of the cliffs. It is not a place for small children.

Below the roadless stretch of the lower canyon, beginning near Agness, a paved highway parallels the river all the way to Gold Beach. Jet boats from Gold Beach regularly carry tourists up the river to Agness and beyond. Some of the longer jet boat trips even travel the white water as far up the river as the Devil's Stairs, a Class III rapid, which has high waves and narrow passages.

Rogue River Ranch

Only one point along the river in the roadless stretch can be reached by car, and that is at **Marial** (see Figure 15), where a gravel road descends to the river from the ridge above. The area was settled by whites in the 1880s, and was named "Marial" after the daughter of early

settlers. The population of the area was as high as 100 people in the early 1900s. In 1970 the property was sold to the Federal government. The ranch buildings, painted red, are today known as the **Rogue River Ranch**, operated by the Bureau of Land Management, and open to the public. The ranch is listed on the National Register of Historic Places. It can reached by car from Glendale on the north side of the canyon, partially on paved and partially on gravel roads. The route is long and winding, and is not open in winter. Ample

Figure 16 - Rogue River Ranch

time should be allowed, and a full fuel tank is essential, because there are no services until Gold Beach.

There also is a road that runs along the ridges to the south of the canyon, from **Galice** to **Agness** (see Figure 15), called the **Bear Camp Road**. The route is paved, but is narrow in places, and has been subject to slides. It is closed by snow in winter. As with the road on the north side, a full fuel tank is essential. In the case of both the roads on the north and on the south, they reach elevations much higher than the river, and it is wise to seek information on road conditions in advance, from the Bureau of Land Management office in Grants Pass.

Zane Grey

Zane Grey, the famous author of western novels, loved the Rogue River, and even wrote a book about it, called *Rogue River Feud.* He returned many times to the river to fish (some people say that fishing was more important to Grey than were his books), and he even maintained a cabin on the river, reachable by pack train. The **Zane Grey Cabin** is still there, and is about midway in the roadless section of the lower canyon.

The story of *Rogue River Feud* is centered in Grants Pass, Gold Beach, and the lower canyon. The time is about 1920, and the hero has just returned from World War I, a broken man, physically and spiritually. The "feud" is between the upriver fishermen and the commercial fishermen on the lower river who use nets with a mesh smaller than is legal, in order to catch undersized fish. The issue is that overfishing at the river mouth is destroying the salmon and steelhead runs up the river, after which the fish would run no more.

The hero becomes involved in the feud, kills a man in self-defense, and has to go into hiding in the canyon, where he falls in love with a beautiful young woman who lives there with her father. The hero is an expert fisherman, buts finds that the beautiful young woman is even better at fishing than he is. After a period of time in which the hero's health and spirit are restored, the two marry, and then the hero finds that his new wife actually is a rich heiress, because her father owns a secret gold mine in the canyon. Along the way, of course, the bad guys are overcome, and the salmon and steelhead are saved.

Zane Grey, as always in his books, does a superlative job in his descriptions of the surroundings in which the action takes place. The first chapter of the book, only four pages long, is a masterful picture of the Rogue River, and of the fish who ascend it to spawn. Clearly, the man who wrote that chapter knew the river and loved it.

Figure 18 - The Applegate Trail

3 The Applegate Trail
"A Southern Route to Oregon"

Peter Skene Ogden

The first whites to reach the Rogue Valley, and who left a written record, were those attached to the 1826-27 expeditions led by Peter Skene Ogden, a chief trader of the Hudson's Bay Company. However, French-Canadian trappers apparently had visited the region earlier, and they were the ones who originated the name "Rogue," because they called the Takelma Indians of the region "*les coquins*", or "the rogues."

In September 1826, Ogden departed from Fort Vancouver, near present-day Portland, traveled east on the Columbia River, then south through central Oregon, and reached the region near Upper Klamath Lake about the first of December. He gave the Klamath River its name, calling it the "Clammitte," and gave the name "Mt. Sastise" to the mountain we know today as Mount McLoughlin.

Figure 17 - OPPOSITE PAGE - Grave marker for Martha Leland Crowley, age 16, near Grave Creek in Sunny Valley

They spent the winter in the region, trapping beaver, and in March 1827, crossed over the Siskiyou Pass into the Rogue Valley. Ogden's journal says, of the Rogue River, ". . . .reached fine large river having crossed the mountains." Ogden called it the "Sastise" River. Also, he apparently believed that the Applegate River, which joins the Rogue at about this point, was the Klamath River. His expedition crossed over into the Umpqua Valley, but his journal says that the Indians told him that the trappers from the Willamette had visited the region and taken all the beaver.

The party then departed over the route by which they had come, over Siskiyou Pass, and then along a route that took them near the Pit River and Goose Lake. When traveling near the Pit River, they encountered some of the pits dug by the local Indians to capture wild animals, and three of Ogden's men, in spite of having been warned by the Indians, accidentally fell into the pits, together with their horses.

The South Road Expedition

Signs placed along I-5 at intervals announce that you are following the route of the Apple-gate Trail. Many people are aware that the trail represented an alternate immigrant route to Oregon, but few know how much suffering was endured by the first immigrants who took the trail.

In 1846, Jesse Applegate and fourteen men, organized into the "South Road Expedition," started from near Portland in an attempt to find a new "southern" route to Oregon as an alternate to the regular Oregon Trail. He shared leadership with another experienced westerner, Levi Scott, and some people believe the trail should be called "The Applegate-Scott Trail."

A major motive for the expedition was to find a route that would avoid the dangers of the rapids of the Columbia River. Previously, on his journey west, Applegate's boat had over-turned in the Columbia River, drowning his son. He wanted a safer route. Another motive for finding a new route was the fear that war between the United States and England was imminent, which would close the route along the Columbia.

The South Road Expedition had a sketchy map of the region through which the South Road would have to pass, based on information from Peter Skene Ogden, and they presumed a satisfactory route could be found. They also knew of statements by Ogden that their route was "infested with fierce and war-like savages," and that the "Rogue River had taken its name from the character of the Indians inhabiting its valleys." Ogden was also reported as saying that it would be impossible to build a road through the country. All of these statements were discounted by the members of the expedition as British propaganda, to discourage Americans from seeking a South Road alternative to the usual Oregon Trail down the Columbia.

Applegate's party followed the Oregon-California Trail (see Page 37), a trail that had occasionally been used by fur trappers since the 1830s. They went south from the Willamette Valley, over the difficult terrain south of Roseburg, to the Rogue River. As they traveled up the Bear Creek Valley, they overtook a band of Hudson's Bay Trappers who told them of a good way to cross the mountains by going east along Emigrant Creek near Ashland.

They went over the pass, more or less following the route of today's Highway 66 over Green Springs Summit. They came to the Klamath River, passed by Lower Klamath Lake, went through the dry, rocky region known today as Devils Garden, and crossed the Warner Mountains into Nevada. Then they had to cross the Black Rock Desert, finding a route with just enough small springs to make their passage possible. After severe difficulties, they finally joined the regular California Trail along the Humboldt River in Nevada, near the place where the river ends in what is called "Humboldt Sink." (Subsequently, when they returned with a group of emigrants, they turned off the California Trail near today's Rye Patch Reservoir, which provided a shorter route across the Black Rock Desert.)

They went on to Fort Hall, located on the main emigrant trail to Oregon, and encouraged those taking that trail to take their new route instead. Emigrants with about 90 wagons decided to take the new trail, ultimately straggling out in small groups over a stretch of more than 50 miles. Jesse Applegate started back along his new trail, ahead of the wagons, to mark the route. Levi Scott remained with the wagons, and was elected as their leader. (Mount Scott in Crater Lake National Park is named for him.) It presumably was understood that the emigrants themselves would have do the work to make the route passable for wagons, but some of the emigrants later severely criticized Applegate for misrepresenting the ease of passage.

It took the emigrants on the new trail from August to December to make it to the Willamette Valley, with many dying along the way, mostly because of illness or accidents. Near Goose Lake, on the Oregon-California border, a group of Indians killed several of their cattle. Then, near Tule Lake, Indians again raided and stole some cattle. A search party was sent out, and a member of the party, spotting an Indian, shot and killed him. The search party found a small village, and, assuming this was the village of the people who had stolen the cattle, destroyed it. The stage thus was set for continuing conflict with the Indians. A few days later, it was discovered that a member of the party had fallen behind and was missing. A search party found his body, with nine arrows in it.

As they proceeded, the emigrants found that they had to cut down trees and construct some kind of rough surface so the wagons could pass. Going over the Cascades was difficult, especially at the steep places known as "Jenny Creek Slide," and "Keene Creek Slide." By the time they got over the Cascades it was October, and they had only gotten as far as the Bear Creek Valley, near Ashland. (It is worth noting that, at about the same time, the ill-fated Donner Party was attempting to climb over the Sierra Nevada mountains in California, only to get trapped by heavy snows for a winter of starvation.)

One might suppose the worst was now over, but the worst actually was yet to come. Passage down the Bear Creek Valley and through the region around Medford was relatively easy, although Indians continued to steal cattle, and one of the emigrants, out of fear, shot an Indian. The result was that Indians shadowed the wagons, occasionally shooting arrows at the emigrants.

The Ordeal of Canyon Creek

The emigrants now tackled the mountains lying between Grants Pass and Roseburg, and here they had their greatest trials. Even though they were on the route of the California-Oregon Pack Trail, it was only that -- a pack trail. It was necessary to construct some kind of road for the wagons, and in the end many had to leave their wagons behind. The worst was in the "Umpqua Canyon," known today as Canyon Creek, where the road had to go directly down the bed of the creek which was now running high with water, because it was November and the rains had come.

Food was running low. A couple of young men in the party were sent ahead on foot, to try to reach the settlements and summon aid. A major problem was to cross the rivers that lay in their way, and many had to leave their wagons behind. Some unloaded their wagons, carried the contents across by canoe, and floated the wagon boxes across. In some cases they were

29

able to pay the Indians for use of their canoes, but in other cases they had to construct their own dugout canoes.

By December, they began to straggle into the lower end of the Willamette Valley, and finally made contact with relief parties coming to their aid. The late ones had to wade through heavy snow, but their ordeal was over. One family decided to remain through the winter at a site near Oakland, Oregon, subsisting on "poor beef and venison," plus "a few roots obtained from the Indians."

As it happened, that very year a treaty was signed between the United States and England, which established the border at its present location, thus removing one of the motives for finding a southern route to Oregon. But this happened while the Applegate Trail emigrants were en route, so they knew nothing of it until they arrived in the Willamette Valley.

Grave Creek and Sunny Valley

Grave Creek is on I-5, about 14 miles north of Grants Pass. The name commemorates the death, of typhoid fever, of a 16-year-old girl named Martha Leland Crowley, who was a member of the first party of emigrants on the Applegate Trail. **The Applegate Trail Interpretive Center** is nearby, and a short distance north of the Interpretive Center there is a grave marker near the site of her burial, next to the modern road. The precise site of her burial is uncertain, because the immigrants had taken precautions to hide the site from Indians, by burying her in the middle of the road and burning brush over the grave. One authority claims the site is actually under the present-day road. Including Martha, seven members of the Crowley family died during the trip to Oregon.

The area of Grave Creek is known today as **Sunny Valley**. Prior to that time, it had been called "Grave Creek House," "Ft. Leland," "Leland," or just "Grave Creek." The reason for the name change apparently was because local residents felt the name "Grave Creek" was too depressing. They chose "Sunny Valley," because the valley is relatively free of the winter fogs which often accumulate in other valleys in Southern Oregon. President Hayes and his party stayed at the Grave Creek House in 1880.

The Green Springs Highway

In later years, the trail over the Green Springs Summit continued to be used to some degree, although traffic fell off in 1849, when thousands of pioneers went to the California gold fields instead of to Oregon. Then, in 1852, after gold was discovered in Jacksonville, traffic over the Green Springs increased. It is claimed that, in 1853, 3500 people took this route.

By the 1860s, traffic was moving in both directions, but the steep "slides" at Jenny Creek and Keene Creek were a vexing problem. Going east to west, they were indeed "slides," but going in the other direction, they represented steep upward climbs. To get up, wagons had to be unloaded and their contents carried upward, while the empty wagons were hauled up. In 1873, the state constructed the Southern Wagon Road, which offered a gentler route. In 1911, an automobile actually negotiated the road, taking 5 days to go from Lakeview to Ashland. In 1919, the construction of today's Highway 66 began, which took several years to complete. **Tub Springs Wayside** (sometimes spelled "Tubb Springs") is a pleasant spot a few miles east of the Greensprings Summit, along the Applegate route. A section of the old trail passes near the springs.

30

Figure 19 - The old wagon road over the Green Springs, near Tub Springs.

A Confusion of Names

To confuse the issue of names, there sometimes is uncertainty as to just what is meant by the term "Applegate Trail." From the Willamette Valley to Ashland, the route coincides with that of the old Oregon-California Pack Trail, and it became the main route for travel between Oregon and California. To many, it is this section that is mostly meant, when the term "Applegate Trail" is used. The **Applegate Trail Interpretive Center** is along this section of trail, in Sunny Valley.

To further confuse matters, the portion of the trail from central Nevada to Goose Lake was used by many emigrants who actually were heading for California, not Oregon, on a route pioneered by Peter Lassen. The "Lassen Cutoff" left the Applegate Trail near Goose Lake, and headed south along the Pit River and into Sacramento Valley. In fact, some people refer to the trail as the "Applegate-Lassen Cutoff."

An interesting sidelight is the origin of the name "Jenny Creek," where the troublesome "Jenny Creek Slide" was located. It is natural to suppose it was named after someone called Jenny, but that's not how it happened. In 1852, when a group of volunteers was chasing Indians, a "jenny" was drowned as they were crossing the creek, and that was the source of its name. (For those who don't already know, a "jenny" is a female donkey.)

4 The Rogue River Indian War

The Takelmas

At the time of the arrival of whites in the Rogue Valley, the main tribe of Indians was known as the Takelmas, who inhabited the Rogue, Applegate, and Illinois watersheds. On the other side of the Siskiyou divide was the Shasta tribe, who were closely related to the Takelmas and spoke essentially the same language. An interesting aspect of the Takelmas and Shastas was that their language was strikingly different from those of surrounding tribes.

The Takelmas lived by hunting, fishing, and gathering, and apparently made no use of agriculture, although they gathered acorns and dug for camas bulbs. Their winter houses were built of frameworks of poles, covered with slabs of cedar bark, and sealed with clay. Two or three families would gather in a winter group. In the summer they would range widely, using temporary shelters. They traded with neighboring tribes for things they did not themselves have, such as obsidian for arrow and spear heads.

Bravery and honesty were esteemed, although stealing from other tribes, or from whites, was permissible. Suicide was looked upon with disfavor, which casts doubt upon legends of Indian maidens casting themselves off cliffs, such as at Table Rocks. Capturing of members of other tribes was a common practice, which generally took the form of carrying off young girls, who usually became members of the tribes of their captors.

It has been estimated that, at the time of the arrival of the whites, there were about 600 members of the tribes and bands that constituted the Takelmas. In 1911, some 60 years after the Takelmas had been defeated in war and moved to a reservation in the north, a government count showed that only 6 of the Takelmas remained.

Discovery of Gold In Oregon

After 1848, and the discovery of gold in California, many people left the Willamette Valley and traveled down the Oregon-California Trail, to get to the California gold fields. In the spring of 1851, a group known as the Rollins Party joined the traffic. When the party reached the Rogue, they met some friendly Indians who traded with them for salmon. When asked about gold in the region, the Indians offered to guide the party "down-river," where they said was much gold.

The Indians guided them over the mountains to the Illinois River. There indeed was gold there, and the creek in which it was found was named Josephine Creek, after a 16-year old girl in the party, Josephine Rollins. Later, the county itself was named Josephine County.

Only a few months later, a greater gold discovery was made in the vicinity of Jacksonville, and the rush was on. Prospectors on the coast even found gold in the beach sands near the mouth of the Rogue River, leading to the name "Gold Beach."

The War Begins

Miners poured into the area, and worked over all the creeks of the Rogue, the Applegate, and the Illinois Rivers, finding gold almost everywhere. Many people returned from California, large numbers traveled down from the Willamette Valley, and others came over a new trail from Crescent City. The latter found gold in the upper Illinois River drainage, and established a camp known as "Sailor Diggings." We know it today as Waldo. It is estimated that the total value of gold found in Southern Oregon in the 1850s was more than $30 million.

As the miners spread over the country, the Indians of the area came under heavy pressure, and increasingly saw the white people as a menace. More and more, the native peoples attacked the interlopers, especially along the trails leading to the Rogue Valley. Killings increased, both of miners, and of Indians.

The miners sent a petition, asking for help, to Major Stephen Kearny, who was known to be approaching the area from the north. Kearny's forces met the Indians near the Table Rocks, and engaged in a number of skirmishes. The battles were inconclusive, but Kearny took a number of women and children prisoners. Governor Gaines arrived in the Rogue Valley at about that time, and sent word for the chiefs to meet with him. Because of the prisoners, the chiefs agreed to peace terms. The prisoners were released, and the governor promised to appoint an agent to look after the needs of the native people. In the peace agreement, the Indians were to stay on the north side of the Rogue River, in the area of the Table Rocks, and the whites were not to bother them.

There followed a period of uneasy "peace." But there were occasional killings, for which the Indians were held responsible, and one miner was killed right on the edge of Jacksonville. The day after that, a miner was shot as he entered his cabin. Groups of volunteers spread over the countryside, and captured a couple of Indians. Since the Indians possessed the same kind of ammunition that had been used in the killings, they were judged guilty, and were hanged.

Rumors abounded that the Indians were getting ready for war. A plea for help from army troops was sent northward, and the miners organized themselves as volunteers, to carry the war to the Indians. The volunteer groups found and demolished an Indian village, but were ambushed the next day, got the worst of it, and retreated to Jacksonville.

At about that time, a group of volunteers from the north arrived, under the command of General Joe Lane. After battles that resulted in a standoff, a peace parley was agreed to. General Lane went alone into the Indian camp, and arranged an armistice. Following the armistice, representatives of both sides met on the slopes of Upper Table Rock, and, after much uncertainty, finally arrived at a treaty.

The Table Rocks Treaty

The treaty, in 1853, provided that most of the land in the Rogue Valley would be ceded to the whites. It also established a reservation for the Indians ten miles square, centered on the Table Rocks, and on the north side of the Rogue River. Chief Sam, for whom Sams Valley* is named, was one of the chiefs who agreed to remain on the reservation. The government was to pay $60,000 for the ceded land, the actual payments to be in the form of such things as blankets, clothing, and agricultural implements. The government also promised that no whites would be allowed to live on the property reserved for the Indians.

Subsequently, further agreements were reached with tribes that had not been parties to the original treaty. However, a major problem was that there still were Indian bands who had not been involved in the treaty, and did not feel bound by it.

---

*The question often comes up, "why not Sam's, instead of Sams"? The policy comes from the U.S. Board of Geographical Names, which states: "Apostrophes suggesting possession or association are not to be used within the body of a proper geographic name (Henrys Fork: not Henry's Fork)."

After the treaty at the Table Rocks, a fort, named Fort Lane, was constructed by the army on the south side of the Rogue River facing Lower Table Rock. The purpose of the fort was not only to control the Indians, but also to control the whites. There is a hard-to-find old stone marker at the site of the fort, on Gold Ray Road near the railroad tracks, 0.7 mile from the intersection of Gold Ray Road and Blackwell Road.

Full-blown War

In spite of the treaty and the fort, trouble continued on both sides, some of it coming from young Indian men attacking pack trains and isolated camps, and some from miners who wanted only for the Indians to be exterminated.

In the fall of 1855, a group of miners from Jacksonville decided to "teach the Indians a lesson." There was a small Indian village near Little Butte Creek, that the miners surrounded at night. At dawn they opened fire, killing eight men, four of them old, and fifteen women and children.

Retaliation was swift. Bands of Indians went on a rampage, attacking settler's cabins, and killing the inhabitants. On the Oregon-California Trail, 16 travelers were killed in one day. Soldiers from Fort Lane checked on Chief Sam's people, but found them to be on their reservation and taking no part in the killings.

A call went out for volunteers, and they came, both from the Willamette Valley in the north, and from Yreka in the south. An army detachment from Port Orford came up the Rogue River in an attempt to find a practical way through the rugged lower gorge. They were unaware of the full-scale hostilities, and ran into a battle with Indians who were coming from the Rogue Valley. The Indians, fighting from good positions, stopped the advance of the soldiers and forced them to withdraw.

Army detachments had started arriving in the Rogue Valley, and late in November, a small force was sent from Fort Lane into the canyon country of the Lower Rogue, where the Indians were hiding. They encountered the Indians in a rugged section of the canyon and fought a battle which ended in a stalemate. The onset of winter brought a temporary reduction in hostilities.

In early 1856, the Indian agent in the Rogue Valley decided that Sam's band, consisting of 153 people, should be moved from the Table Rocks Reservation to a new reservation far to the north, in the Grande Ronde Valley. The Indians were promised that when the war was over they could return to the Table Rocks, but it never happened.

Fighting in the Lower Canyon

Also early in 1856, the miners at Gold Beach (then called Ellensburg) were attacked by Indians, most of whom were from coastal tribes. Many of the miners and their families were killed, and a small group took refuge in a makeshift fort they called "Fort Miner." These held off their attackers for 35 days, until rescued by a military column that marched north from Crescent City.

As soon as winter passed, the Indians hiding in the lower canyon of the Rogue decided to take the offensive back to the upper valleys. Major clashes occurred, especially in the Illinois Valley. Whenever troops of soldiers and volunteers attempted to pin a group of Indians down, the Indians would fade away, only to attack again in another place. Finally the Indians withdrew once more into the rugged lower canyon of the Rogue River.

The military forces in the Rogue Valley by this time numbered about 600 men, mostly volunteers. They launched a mission down the lower canyon, with troops on the ridges on both sides of the river, hoping to catch the Indians between them. An Indian camp was found, and a battle was fought, ending when the Indians withdrew further down the river.

Because of the difficult terrain along the Lower Rogue, an army detachment headed for the coast via an alternate route along the Illinois River. The found a good trail, showing that this was the best route. As they reached the confluence of the Illinois and Rogue, they came across a fairly large Indian village which had just been vacated. This they destroyed. A month later, a series of attacks on an Indian stronghold about 15 miles upstream from the mouth of the Rogue produced a significant victory for the soldiers.

A new attempt was made to bring about peace, at Oak Flat, a few miles up the Illinois River from its confluence with the Rogue. The coastal Indians agreed to the terms being offered, because they were exhausted by living under difficult conditions through the previous winter, constantly short of rations. They agreed, even though the principal condition was that they would have to move to a reservation. However, many of the Indians from the upper Rogue country did not agree, and vowed to continue fighting.

A troop of 80 soldiers moved from Oak Flat to Big Bend on the Rogue River, where there was a large and open meadow. It seemed to be a suitable place for gathering those who had agreed to surrender. Today, it is a lovely and tranquil spot, but it became the site of the most bitterly fought battle of the war.

As the soldiers were setting up camp, they received word that a large number of the Rogues, perhaps several hundred, were gathering for an attack, instead of surrendering. Upon receipt of this news, the soldiers moved to a wooded knoll nearby, which appeared to provide a good defensive position.

The next morning, the Indians attacked in force, and the soldiers became aware that their "defensive position" was in fact a trap. The battle continued without letup during the day, and the situation of the soldiers became steadily more desperate. The next day brought a continuation of the fighting, and the Indians were on the verge of winning a major battle when the sudden arrival of army reinforcements changed everything.

The Indians retreated up the canyon, but encountered new army troops moving down. They were caught in between, and were dismayed by the sight of so many soldiers. Most of them, realizing this was the end, decided to surrender. In addition to the shock of encountering so many troops, they were suffering from undernourishment, and were in wretched condition. The prisoners, under army guard, were taken to Port Orford, and then to the reservation at Grande Ronde. There were well over a thousand of them, including those belonging to both the coastal and the inland tribes.

5 Stagecoaches, Railroads, & Highways
The "Big Road," the O&C, and the Pacific Highway

The Oregon-California Pack Trail

The Rogue Valley, in the early years, was isolated from the rest of the Pacific Coast because of the mountains on all sides. The route directly up the Rogue River from the sea was considered impossible, because of the narrow canyon through the rugged Coast Range. Even today, that route has no road, although there is a foot trail along the river. Such roads as exist in that region today pretty much keep to the high ridges to the north and south of the river.

The route from the north into the Rogue Valley had to pass over the mountain ranges separating the Willamette Valley from the Rogue, especially through the Umpqua Canyon, as described in the section **The Applegate Trail.** To the east were the high Cascades, and to the south, the Siskiyous. If gold had not been discovered in 1852, the region probably would have continued to be isolated much longer than it was.

Between 1825 and 1843, trappers and traders used the route down through the Willamette Valley and over the Siskiyou Pass, on a trail known as the Hudson Bay Company Pack Trail, the Oregon-California Pack Trail, or the Siskiyou Trail. In 1834, Ewing Young went to California and brought back a herd of horses north over the trail. Three years later he repeated the journey, this time with a large herd of cattle. But it was basically a pack trail and not a wagon road. Even the labor the Applegate Party had put into it, in trying to take their wagons through, had not created a usable road.

The Military Road

In 1853, at least in part because of the conflict with the Rogue River Indians, Congress allocated $20,000 to improve the trail, and to build a military road from the Willamette Valley, through the Rogue Valley and to points south. The road was important, because it was the only form of inland communication between the settlements on the Columbia River and California. The alternative was to take passage by ship from Portland to San Francisco, which could be hazardous in bad weather.

The most difficult parts were through the infamous Umpqua Canyon, over the mountain passes just to the south of it, and over the Siskiyou summit. The part over the Siskiyou summit was a special problem because of the heavy winter snows. The result of the military construction was an improvement, but the road was still generally impassable in winter.

The growth of the population meant that a better means of travel was needed for more than just military purposes. Money for a better road was appropriated ($60,000), and by 1858 a good road had been constructed, over which it was claimed a buggy could be driven. For many years the part over the Siskiyous was operated as a toll road, and teams of oxen were used in the winter to try to keep the snow packed down so it could be traveled.

It was time for a stage company, and the road became known as the "Big Road".

Figure 20 - OPPOSITE PAGE - The Rock Point Station near Gold Hill, constructed in 1865, now remodeled as a tasting room for Del Rio Vineyards.

The Oregon-California Stage Company

Beginning in 1860, and continuing until the railroad came 27 years later, the California Stage Company (later, called the Oregon-California Stage Company) operated between Sacramento and Portland. The 710 miles could be covered in about 7 days in the summer ("short time"), but longer in winter ("long time"). The fare was 10 cents per mile, later raised to 15 cents.

Stage stations were spaced 10 or 12 miles apart, where horses could be changed. In the immediate region of the Rogue Valley there were stops in Cottonwood Valley on the California side of Siskiyou Pass, at Barron's near present-day Emigrant Lake, Ashland, Phoenix, Jacksonville, Rock Point near Gold Hill, Grants Pass, Grave Creek in Sunny Valley, Cow Creek near Glendale, and Canyonville. The stage route didn't go through Medford, because the city didn't exist yet. To the north of Jacksonville, there are signs marking the old stage road.

Some of the old stage stations are still there, such as the station at Rock Point, two miles west of Gold Hill on old Highway 99. This station, known as the **Rock Point Hotel** (Figure 20), is on the National Register of Historic Places. The hotel dates from 1865, but it closed in about 1900. In recent years it has been restored, and opened to the public as a tasting room for the nearby Del Rio Vineyards.

The **U.S. Hotel**, a major historic structure in Jacksonville, dates from this period. The famous **Wolf Creek Tavern**, a few miles north of Grave Creek, was not built until 1883, more than 20 years after the stage coaches began to run.

The stages ran day and night, their way at night illuminated by candle lanterns with reflectors. Some passengers went straight through with only rest stops, while others would stay overnight at a station and take their chances on getting a seat the next day.

The road may have been such that "a buggy could be driven on it," but it could be risky in wet weather. The major rivers had bridges, but the lesser creeks were forded. In winter they could be dangerous. The road sometimes became excessively muddy, there were frequent washouts, and there were always the possibilities of runaways, of failed brakes on steep grades, or overturning. Sometimes, if the going became difficult for the horses, the passengers had to get out and walk. It could be a hard passage, but the stages usually went through, nonetheless.

A problem for the stages, of course, were robberies. The stages often carried gold dust, nuggets, coin, currency, and drafts, locked in the famous "green boxes" of the Wells Fargo Company. Generally, there was a Wells Fargo guard on board, "riding shotgun." A favorite technique of the robbers was to stop a stage when the horses were going up a steep grade at a walk, often at night. The steep hills over the Siskiyous were a frequent site of such robberies. In the 14-year period from 1870 to 1884 there were 314 stage robberies. But there were also 206 convictions of the robbers, because of the efforts of Wells Fargo detectives.

Oregon and California Railroad Company (O&C)

Beginning in 1870, the Oregon and California Railroad Company began building its tracks south from Portland, and north from Sacramento. As the railroad advanced, the section served by stagecoaches accordingly shrank. By 1872 the railroad had reached as far south as

Roseburg and as far north as Redding, in California, but stalled there for about 10 years because of financial troubles.

The railroad was reorganized. Southern Pacific Railroad Company assumed management of the system under a lease, and took full ownership some years later. By 1883 the rails from the north had reached Grants Pass, and by 1884 they had come to Phoenix and Ashland, bypassing Jacksonville in the process, causing consternation in that town. The railroad was routed through Medford because of easier grades on that route. Also, Medford was the shortest way to Siskiyou Pass, directly up the Bear Creek Valley. In December 1887, the railroad was complete, with the driving of a golden spike in Ashland. The stagecoach era was over.

The route over the Siskiyou summit was difficult, with many trestles and tunnels. Tunnel 13, which passes under the summit, was 3,108 feet long. The maximum grade was 3.67 percent, which required the use of six "helper" locomotives. In 1992, Southern Pacific shut down the operation over the Siskiyous, and shifted its trains to what was called the "Natron cutoff," which branched off near Weed, California, and went via Klamath Falls and over the Willamette Pass to Eugene. The new route was 23 miles shorter, and had a maximum grade of only 2.2 percent. The change meant that shippers from the Rogue Valley, who wanted to send their goods by rail to California, now had to route them north to Eugene, and then south through Klamath Falls.

Enter the Central Oregon and Pacific Railroad (CORP), which acquired the Southern Pacific tracks over the Siskiyou Pass, and began operation in 1994. Shippers in the Rogue Valley again had a direct route to California, without having to go north through Eugene. CORP carried freight only, and no passenger traffic was involved. Then, in 2003, calamity struck, when vandals set fire to the wooden tunnel supports in Tunnel 13, causing parts of it to collapse. Traffic was halted for almost two years while the tunnel was rebuilt at a cost of $18 million. During that time, freight to and from the Rogue Valley either had to go by truck over I-5, or once more had to take the long detour through Eugene.

As with any railroad, there were train wrecks. The most disastrous wreck the railroad over the Siskiyous ever experienced occurred in July, 1906. A freight train lost its brakes and became a runaway, racing down the grade between the summit and Ashland, jumping its tracks about 5 miles before getting to Ashland, and piling into a jumbled mass. The engineer and one of the brakemen were killed, and another brakeman was severely injured. Two tramps who had been riding the rods survived the wreck without serious injury.

The Great Train Robbery

The infamous Tunnel 13, which burned in 2003, was also the scene of one of the most brutal of train robberies, in October 1923. Tunnel 13 was chosen for the site of the robbery, because it is at the summit of the Siskiyous. A train coming from the north, having climbed the steep grade from Ashland, would stop just before the tunnel to uncouple its "helper" locomotives, and to test its brakes for the downhill run ahead. Thus, as it was entering the tunnel, it was going slowly. Two of the robbers were able to jump aboard the tender at this point. A third robber waited at the other end of the tunnel, bearing dynamite to blast open the mail car, where they expected to find a lot of money.

The two robbers who had jumped the train climbed over the tender and into the cab, and ordered the engineer, at gun point, to stop the train at the opposite end of the tunnel. This the engineer did. He was then ordered, along with the fireman, to get out of the cab and stand by

39

the track. The robber with the dynamite planted his load next to the door of the mail car and detonated it. The explosion ruptured the mail car, killing the clerk inside, and started a fire.

One of the robbers set about trying to get the mail car unhooked from the rest of the train, and then was surprised to discover the brakeman coming toward him, to see why the train was stopped. The brakeman was ordered to continue forward. When he appeared at the front of the train, the two other robbers shot and killed him. Two of the robbers went back to the mail car, to try to get the money they believed to be there, but could see nothing because of the smoke and destruction, and had to give it up. They then returned to the front of the train, where they shot and killed the engineer and fireman. They decided they had to make their getaway, so they headed for a cabin hideout a couple of miles away, that had been prepared in advance.

At this point the train's conductor appeared on the scene, coming forward to investigate the explosion. As soon as he discovered what had happened, he used an emergency phone near the tunnel, to call for help. As a result, one of the "helper" locomotives that had been sitting at the opposite end of the tunnel started into the smoke-filled tunnel to rescue the passengers on the train.

The robbers were three brothers: Roy, Ray, and Hugh D'Autremont. Roy and Ray were twins, 23 years old; Hugh was 19. They stayed for more than two weeks in their hideout. Then, because they were running low on food, Ray hiked back to the tunnel, hopped onto a slowly moving train, and got off at Medford. There, he was astonished to find his picture and one of his brothers on the front page of a newspaper.

The D'Autremonts had been identified because of certain items, such as bib overalls, knapsacks, and a handgun, that they had left behind in the woods during their escape. A crucial bit of evidence was a receipt for registered mail that was found in a pocket of the overalls, that led directly to Roy.

After getting some food in Medford, Ray again jumped aboard a freight train and returned to the hideout. Fearful of the search they knew was under way, they went on foot by a circuitous route to the tracks well south of the tunnel, split up, and jumped on trains, like any hobos. Roy and Ray eventually found their way to Ohio. They adopted assumed names, and attempted to change their appearances, but eventually were recognized from the "wanted" posters, and were captured.

Hugh, also under a different name, and after wandering through several states, enlisted in the army. He was sent to the Phillipines, and was recognized by his sergeant, again from the "wanted" posters. He was apprehended and sent back to the States.

Hugh went to trial first, was found guilty, and was sentenced to life imprisonment. The twin brothers then decided to plead guilty, gave full confessions, and were also sentenced to life imprisonment. Hugh served for 31 years, and was then paroled. He died of cancer 81 days after his parole. Roy was judged mentally incompetent, was sent to a hospital for the insane, and died in a nursing home in 1983. Ray served for 34 years, was paroled in 1961, and died in 1984.

The O&C Lands

After the Civil War, Congress awarded land grants to stimulate the construction of railroads. In 1866, the State of Oregon received a grant of every other square mile, on land stretching from Portland to California, in a band 40 miles wide. Oregon then awarded the grants to the Oregon and California Railroad Company (O&C), to build a railroad. The O&C

began building, but soon violated the stipulations on the land grants, which included requirements that bona fide settlers must settle the land, that the limit to one settler was 160 acres, and the price could not exceed $2.50 an acre.

Because of the violations, the U.S. Congress took back the lands to federal ownership. The railroad (the owner was now the Southern Pacific Railroad) sued, and the case dragged on for years. It finally reached the U.S. Supreme Court, where the railroad lost. Congress then gave the lands to the General Lands Office to manage, and, in 1946 the General Lands Office became the Bureau of Land Management (BLM). Thus, the BLM wound up with millions of acres of forest land, and today the peculiar checkerboard pattern of ownership is visible on maps. They are still referred to as "O&C Lands.".

Rogue River Valley Railway Company

Having been bypassed by the California and Oregon Railway, the citizens of Jacksonville decided to create their own railroad, connecting Jacksonville to Medford. In 1891 the Rogue River Valley Railway Company completed such a line, and continued operations through 1915 under one name or another, carrying mail, freight, and passengers between the two cities. In 1916, the railroad was electrified, as an extension of a streetcar system that had been inaugurated in Medford.

For a few years, the streetcar system and its extension to Jacksonville operated, successfully at first, and then with increasing difficulty because of costly maintenance problems. and the increasing popularity of automobiles. It ceased operation in 1924.

Medco

In 1904, a group of investors announced the construction of a railroad which would go from Medford to Eagle Point, Butte Falls, Crater Lake, "and beyond." It was to be called the **Medford and Crater Lake Railroad.** The railroad got almost to Eagle Point, ran into construction difficulties, and stopped.

The line was bought out and rechristened the Pacific and Eastern Railway. The rails were completed to Butte Falls, and the railroad carried passengers and freight until World War I, after which it closed down. Then the line was purchased by the Medford Logging Railroad Company, after which it became a major carrier of logs from the Butte Falls area to a mill in Medford. During the depression of the 1930s the mill was reorganized as the **Medford Corporation (Medco).** The railroad operated until 1962, after which it was phased out and replaced with trucks.

Oregon and California Coast Railroad

For many years, citizens of both Grants Pass and Crescent City, in California, had dreamed of a railroad linking their cities. Money was subscribed, and a 14-mile section was completed in 1917, from Grants Pass to a point south of Wilderville. This is as far as the railroad ever went. It operated over that short distance with sporadic freight and passenger traffic. But it was unable to compete with Highway 199, which was commissioned in 1926, and even today is the only route between Grants Pass and Crescent City. Then, high water caused the railroad bridge over the Rogue River to collapse, and the line came to an end.

Figure 21 - The "loop" on old Pacific Highway, constructed in 1914. After the cars (seen in the photo) cross over the bridge, they will loop around and go under the same bridge, paralleling the railroad track. The bridge is still in use. (Southern Oregon Historical Society photo #13159)

U.S. 99, the "Pacific Highway"

In the early 1920s, the wagon road through the Rogue Valley and over the Siskiyous became a part of the **Pacific Highway,** extending from Canada to Mexico. In 1926, it was designated as U.S. route 99, as part of a 2-lane paved highway extending from border to border. It was the main north-south route on the Pacific Coast. In parts of California, sections of it were called the "Golden State Route," or the "Ridge Route," but in Oregon it continued to be called the "Pacific Highway." In fact, it is still called that in some of the places where the original highway remains in use.

As was common with most highways in those days, Highway 99 was routed right through the towns and cities along the way, so travelers had to cope with traffic and stop signals. By the 1970s, Highway 99 was superseded by I-5, which offered a multiple-lane route from Canada to Mexico without a traffic signal.

Much of old Highway 99 is still in use, although expanded to four lanes in some places. From Grants Pass to Gold Hill and beyond, it follows the Rogue River closely, and is called the Rogue River Highway. From Central Point to Ashland, it is a heavily used local highway, and portions of it are called "Pacific Highway," as was the whole highway in the Northwest in former times. After Ashland, the old highway picks up again at a point where State Highway 66 passes near the upper end of Emigrant Lake. From Emigrant Lake, it can be followed up to Siskiyou Summit and beyond.

Some of the old road is now buried under Emigrant Lake, but the part that remains is a delightful old two-lane road, twisting its way among the trees. It is delightful now, with light traffic, but in your imagination you can picture it when it was jammed with cars and slow trucks, grinding up the grade ahead of you. (I don't have to imagine it, because I drove over it more than once when it was the only route.) At one point, the highway loops around and crosses over itself on a bridge, also crossing the railroad track. (See Fig. 21.) At the summit, the old road passes under the freeway near the Mount Ashland road and goes over the mountains more or less paralleling I-5, and finally rejoins the freeway near Hilt.

Even though I-5 is a modern four-lane freeway, the pass at **Siskiyou Summit** in wintertime can be a trial. (This pass is often called "Siskiyou Pass," but the "official" Siskiyou Pass is on Old Highway 99, a mile or so to the east of Siskiyou Summit.) Siskiyou Summit is the highest point reached anywhere along I-5, at 4,310 feet. The portion from the summit to Ashland has grades of six percent, and curves sharp enough to require a reduction in speed. In winter, the route over the summit can get tough, and is occasionally closed because of ice and snow, or because of an accident. Tire chains are often required.

Sometimes, motorists going south, relieved to find they have negotiated Siskiyou Summit successfully, are dismayed to discover they must travel over a similar summit, with similar weather problems, when they get to **Black Butte Summit** (3,934 feet) near Mount Shasta City.

Figure 23 - Southern Cascades, with Mount McLoughlin in distance

6 The Mountains Around Us

The Mountains

In the first chapter, I said that one of the attractive features of the Rogue Valley is the manner in which it is surrounded by forested mountains. Anywhere you stand in the valley, you can look up and see them. Furthermore, they are likely to remain much the way they look today, because they are mostly in Federal ownership, and thus belong to all the people. They can be considered to have three parts -- the Cascades, the Siskiyous, and the Rogue-Umpqua Divide. The eastern part of the Rogue-Umpqua Divide belongs to the Western Cascades, while the western part merges into the Coast Range.

Figure 22 - OPPOSITE PAGE - Golden-mantled Ground Squirrel at Crater Lake

The Cascades

Oregon is strongly identified with the Cascade Range, which is distinguished by a chain of lofty, lovely volcanoes, including Mount Hood in the north, Oregon's highest peak at 11,239 ft. In Southern Oregon, the major volcanoes are Mount Mazama, which holds Crater Lake, and Mount McLoughlin. Farther south, in California, the Cascade Range is dominated by Mount Shasta, at 14,162 ft., and finally comes to an end with Lassen Peak.

In Jackson County, after the Cascades reach a high point at Mount McLoughlin, they turn sharply to the west, and wind up forming the forested ridge visible to the east of Ashland. At Green Springs Summit, where Highway 66 crosses, it is generally accepted that the Cascade Crest is interrupted at that point, and that the east-west range just to the south is a part of the Siskiyous (see below). But we know that the Cascades really don't end at Green Springs Summit, because Shasta and Lassen, to the south, are indisputably part of the Cascades. What happens in between? Where do the Cascades go from Green Springs Summit?

The answer is not clear-cut. All the way from the Columbia River, the Cascades exist as an unbroken mountain range. But now, looking to the south, into California, the range is cut through by the Klamath River, separating Mount Shasta from its northern sisters. Farther south is Mount Lassen, also set off by itself because of rivers. So, from Green Springs Summit to the south, the Cascades do not exist as an unbroken mountain crest, but as more or less isolated mountains.

The Siskiyou Mountains

The Siskiyous are unusual among North American mountain ranges, because they run roughly parallel to the Oregon-California state line, east to west, inside of north to south. They are a part of the larger region known as the Klamath Mountains, which includes the Trinity Mountains, the Marble Mountains, and the Salmon Mountains. All of the latter three are entirely within California, but the Siskiyous are about evenly divided between the two states. Their western edge is at the Pacific Ocean; and on the east they extend beyond Soda Mountain, and end at Jenny Creek. Through most of Josephine and Jackson Counties, their northern boundary is the Rogue River, but eastward from Ashland, the northern boundary is more or less Highway 66. The highest peak in the range is Mount Ashland, at 7532 ft.

The Klamath Mountains, including the Siskiyous, are often referred to as the "Klamath Knot," because of the manner in which layer upon layer of rock layers have been pushed by continental forces into what has been called "a hopelessly confused heap." The complicated geology has produced a complex set of habitats, with the result that many plant species grow only here and nowhere else. A factor is that there are many areas of a rock called **serpentine**, which is deficient in some minerals, and high in others that are toxic to some plants. Thus, the species that grow in serpentine areas tend to be very specialized. In 1992, the World Conservation Union classified the Klamath-Siskiyou region as an "Area of Global Botanical Significance."

The Rogue-Umpqua Divide

The relatively low line of forested mountains to the north of the Rogue Valley is the Rogue-Umpqua Divide. In the west, the high points of the range are about 4000 to 5000 ft.

high, but I-5 crosses it at Stage Road Pass, at about 1820 feet, when it passes from the Wolf Creek drainage (belonging to the Rogue River) to the Cow Creek drainage (belonging to the Umpqua River). A high point in this region is **King Mountain** (5253 feet), about 18 miles to the north of Grants Pass. A road that is partly paved and partly gravel goes from Wolf Creek to the summit of King Mountain.

Another place where a paved road crosses over the divide, at an elevation of about 3300 feet, is on the road from Trail to Tiller, north of Shady Cove. Another crossing is where OR 230, the highway from Medford to Diamond Lake, goes over the divide at 5415 feet, close to Crater Lake, and this is where the Rogue-Umpqua Divide meets the High Cascades. Much of the country along the divide has been designated as the **Rogue-Umpqua Divide Wilderness.**

Figure 24 - Pacific Crest Trail near Pilot Rock

Pacific Crest Trail

The Pacific Crest Trail, known affectionately as the **PCT**, is 2,600 miles long, extending from Mexico to Canada. Some people (so-called "through-hikers") have traveled the entire length in one season, which takes about six months. Others have done it in stages. Even more have just done selected sections of it. In our own region, the trail is so accessible that many people use it for day-hikes. With regard to through-hikers, the guidebook *Pacific Crest Trail* says that if you pass through the Sky Lakes Wilderness, near Mount McLoughlin, before late July, the mosquitoes "will drive you almost insane."

The PCT travels through the high country to the south and east of the Rogue Valley, and generally does not offer mosquito concentrations to equal those reputed to be in the Sky Lakes Wilderness. The trail passes from California to Oregon near Dutchman Peak, and then more or less parallels the Siskiyou Crest Road, through magnificent subalpine country, as far as Mount Ashland. In this region, it is accessible at many points along Forest Road 20 (gravel), and is heavily used by day-hikers. (See Page 56.)

From Mount Ashland, it descends and passes under I-5 near Siskiyou Summit, following old Highway 99. Then it ascends to the Siskiyou Crest once more, passes near Pilot Rock in the Cascade-Siskiyou National Monument, and emerges at Green Springs Summit, on OR 66. It is easily accessible at Pilot Rock and from the Soda Springs Road. This is another area heavily favored by day-hikers. (See Page 53.)

Figure 25 - On top of Lower Table Rock

From Green Springs Summit it heads north, passing near both Hyatt and Howard Prairie Lakes. Sections of the trail are easily accessible from the gravel road that goes north from Green Springs Summit, called Little Hyatt Lake Road, and this part is also popular with day-hikers.

Another place where the trail crosses a main highway is near the Jackson County/ Klamath County border, on Dead Indian Memorial Road. At OR 140, it crosses near Fish Lake. The resort and campground at Fish Lake are often used by through-hikers for a brief stay in more or less civilized surroundings. Then it enters the Sky Lake Wilderness (with its mosquitoes). After Sky Lakes, the trail enters Crater Lake National Park, and crosses OR 62 inside the park. After traversing Crater Lake National Park, it leaves our area.

Table Rocks

The Table Rocks are highly visible landmarks in the Rogue Valley, and seem more appropriate to the deserts of the southwest than to Oregon. They are often referred to as "islands in the sky," a descriptive term that seems just right.

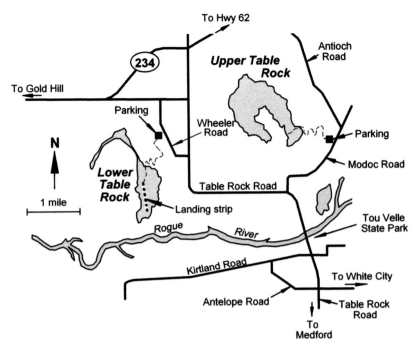

Figure 26 - The Table Rocks

Some have speculated that the rocks are the old cores of volcanic plugs, but the explanation is quite different. About 7 million years ago, lava apparently erupted near Lost Creek Lake, flowed down the valley of the Rogue River, and solidified into a sheet. Erosion then went to work, finding ways to eat away at the softer layers under the lava, but leaving portions of the harder lava cap. Finally, only two remnants of the lava sheets remained, as the two Table Rocks.

A public trail to Upper Table Rock was created in the 1970s, and to Lower Table Rock in the 1980s. The trails are managed by The Nature Conservancy (TNC) and the Bureau of Land Management (BLM).

The rocks are beloved by Rogue Valley residents, and an estimated 10,000 people climb them every year. The hikes are classed as moderate, ranging from two miles to three miles (round trip), with an elevation gain in each case of 700 to 800 feet. April is the most popular month, because this is when most of the flowers are out, and when the birds are most active.

To get to the rocks from Medford, go north on Highway 62, 5.8 miles to Antelope Road, and turn west. Go 1.8 miles on Antelope Road to Table Rock Road and turn right (north). To get to **Upper Table Rock,** turn right (east) on Modoc Road, which is 1.8 miles north of Antelope Road, and follow signs to the parking lot. To get to **Lower Table Rock,** continue on Table Rock Road to Wheeler Road (4.2 miles from Antelope Road). Turn left (west) on Wheeler Road and follow signs to the parking lot.

Upper Table Rock is indeed slightly higher in elevation than Lower Table Rock, at 2091 feet as opposed to 2049 feet. However, Upper Table Rock actually got its name because it is more upstream along the Rogue River than is Lower Table Rock.

The two trails lead through oak savanna and brushy ceanothus/manzanita areas at the beginning, then through denser forests of madrone and Douglas-fir, and finally onto the open tops. The trails are suitable for family groups, although there are steep places where people should be careful, and poison oak is abundant. The trails are noted for their wildflowers in spring.

The views of the Rogue Valley from the tops of both rocks merit the use of a major word: *stunning*. (See photo facing title page.) It is possible to find a secluded perch on the edge of the cliffs, and gaze at the valley below, with Mount McLoughlin in the distance. On Lower Table Rock, you can walk across the level surface on the old abandoned air strip, clear to the opposite side. The airstrip, until about 1990, was used mostly for recreational purposes by builders of experimental home-built aircraft, but is now returning to a more natural state.

On Upper Table Rock the walk across the top is shorter, and takes you to the edge of the bowl-shaped canyon in the middle. The canyon itself is off limits, but you can sit on the edge in spring and listen to the canyon wrens singing below.

The Prairies and the Lakes

In Colorado, the vast mountain meadows are called "parks." In our part of the west they are often called "prairies," and Southern Oregon has lots of them. One of the best -- Howard Prairie -- is perched at an elevation of almost 5000 feet in the mountains above Ashland.

The main access road from the Rogue Valley is **Dead Indian Memorial Road.** The name apparently got its start in 1854, when the bodies of two Indians were discovered in deserted shelters along a small creek that drains Howard Prairie. The Indians apparently had been murdered, and Klamath Indians were blamed for the deed. The creek was subsequently called "Dead Indian Creek," and appears under that name on the topographic map of the area. The surrounding region was called "Dead Indian Country," or, sometimes, "Dead Indian Plateau."

A trail through the region was an established trade route of the Indians, and the white settlers soon converted the trail to a wagon road. At first, the road was called "Indian Market Road," and later, it became "Dead Indian Road." In 1993, Jackson County, recognizing the negative connotations associated with the name "Dead Indian Road," officially changed it to "Dead Indian Memorial Road."

From Ashland, go east on Dead Indian Memorial Road about 16 miles, to the magnificent view of the great meadows of **Howard Prairie**, with Mount McLoughlin in the background. In June, portions of the prairie turn a bluish color with common camas. Most of the mountain prairies in this region get varying amounts of camas in spring, and in some instances the blue camas flowers can be so dense that the meadows are sometimes mistaken for lakes.

An interesting question that arises here is: just where, exactly, is the Cascade crest? It turns out that this question has a surprisingly complex answer. Before humans began altering the flow of water courses, the high point over which Dead Indian Memorial Road passes was *not* the Cascade crest. Today, it is. What happened?

As you are heading east, the stream that runs parallel to Dead Indian Memorial Road on your right, after crossing the summit, is Dead Indian Creek. Left to its own devices, the creek would intersect the road just about where the flattest part of Howard Prairie begins, would run under the road, and then down to the north, eventually to empty into the Rogue River. Thus, under those circumstances, the crest would lie along the ridge to the south of Dead Indian Creek.

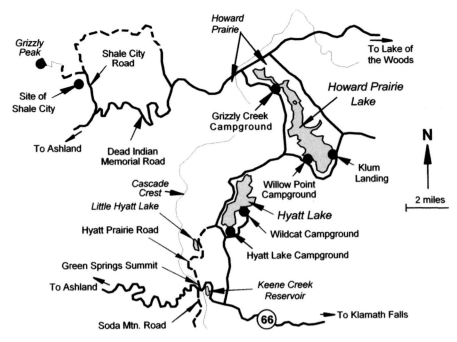

Figure 27 - Howard Prairie and Hyatt Lakes

But, just where the stream meets the road, there is a diversion dam that interrupts its historical flow, and instead sends the water from Dead Indian Creek through a ditch into **Howard Prairie Lake.** Howard Prairie Lake drains into the Klamath River, so the flow from Dead Indian Creek now belongs to the Klamath drainage, instead of to the Rogue. As a consequence of this diversion, the crest is now the high point you came over on Dead Indian Memorial Road.

After you pass the diversion dam, and are on the more or less flat surface of Howard Prairie, you come to a point where the water on one side of you flows to the east, and on the other side, to the west. Thus, at this one point at least, Howard Prairie itself is the Cascade crest, a most un-crestlike state of affairs.

Beyond Howard Prairie, the crest shifts back and forth on either side of Dead Indian Memorial Road, until finally, near Lake of the Woods, it heads north toward Mount McLoughlin. At this point it starts behaving like a major mountain divide is supposed to. (For more on the diversion of water in this region, see page 83.)

Not far beyond the diversion dam -- the one that changed the location of the "crest" -- is Hyatt Prairie Road, on the right. Howard Prairie Recreation Area, with a marina, store, and campground, lies about three miles down this road, and Hyatt Lake (see chapter on Cascade-Siskiyou National Monument) is three miles further. Along the road between the two lakes are numerous small aspen-lined meadows. The aspens are a lovely green in the spring, and an even more lovely yellow in the fall.

A bird that can usually be found at Howard Prairie Lake or at nearby Hyatt Lake, is the bald eagle. One might be perched in a dead tree along the shore, or might be in the forest on the opposite side of the lake. Scan the trees on the other side of one of the lakes for a white spot that seems to be out of place. When binoculars are focused on such a white spot, the spot often turns out to be the head of a bald eagle.

The **Rogue Yacht Club,** based in Medford, emphasizes sailing, conducts sailing classes, and has a summer racing schedule, primarily at Howard Prairie Lake. The biggest event of the year is the **Howard Prairie Regatta,** held annually the last weekend in July. Any person of good character who is interested in sailing can join the Rogue Yacht Club. It's not even necessary to own a boat.

In winter, the Bureau of Land Management manages ski trails and snowmobile trails in the mountains to the west of Howard Prairie and Hyatt Lakes, referred to as the **Buck Prairie Winter Recreation Area.** Access points are on Dead Indian Memorial Road, and near Hyatt Lake.

Grizzly Peak

Figure 28 - At the Howard Prairie Regatta

From Ashland, Grizzly Peak is highly visible to the northeast. The trail to the summit is highly popular, and involves a round trip hike of about four miles. To get to the trail, go on Dead Indian Memorial Road about 7 miles from Ashland to Shale City Road, on the left. It is 2.9 miles on Shale City Road to the gravel road that leads to the Grizzly Peak trailhead.

The Grizzly Peak trail runs through beautiful forest, but bypasses the true summit, which is rather obscure. It terminates at a point marked "Grizzly, 5747 feet" on the map, that overlooks Ashland. This is the point that people generally label as "Grizzly Peak" when it is seen from below. Toward the end of the trail, there are many burned trees, the result of the East Antelope Fire of 2002.

Grizzly Peak is named for "Old Reelfoot" a grizzly bear that inhabited the region. The bear was killed in 1890, and was reported to be the last grizzly in Southern Oregon.

Shale City

Not far from Ashland, close to Grizzly Peak, there is a deposit of **oil shale.** Oil shale is a fine-grained rock containing organic matter, from which a type of crude oil can be obtained by crushing and heating the rock, and then by distilling the vapors. The Grizzly Peak deposit is said to be the only such deposit in Oregon, and is of good commercial quality. However, the recovery process is expensive, and the deposit is so limited in extent that it is not considered economical to recover.

Nevertheless, in the 1920s there was an attempt to do so. A company was formed, some people were hired and they built some cabins, which were called "Shale City." Some rock was mined, crushed, and heated, but it was disappointing, and the promoters disappeared. The area was mostly abandoned. All that remains of Shale City today is an excavation, about ½ mile southwest of the road that leads to the Grizzly Peak Trail. The site is privately owned, and not accessible to the public, with a locked gate and a "no trespassing" sign.

Cascade-Siskiyou National Monument

The Presidential Proclamation that created Cascade-Siskiyou National Monument said, in part:

> With towering fir forests, sunlit oak groves, wildflower-strewn meadows, and steep canyons, the Cascade-Sisikiyou National Monument is an ecological wonder, with biological diversity unmatched in the Cascade Range. This rich enclave of natural resources is a biological crossroads -- the interface of the Cascade, Klamath, and Siskiyou ecoregions, in an area of unique geology, biology, climate, and topography.

Green Springs Summit (see map, Figure 27) lies just about at the center of the monument, and this is where the Cascades and the Siskiyous meet. As a result, plant and bird species that are typical of those two mountain ranges mingle in the monument. Also, Great Basin species such as western juniper, big sagebrush, and plains prickly pear cactus even show up. Spotting specimens of juniper and sagebrush might not be difficult, but don't bother looking for the prickly pear cactus, because it's in a remote, hard-to-reach part of the monument.

A map of the monument in places has a checkerboard appearance, because it consists of 53,000 acres of federal land, managed by the Bureau of Land Management (BLM), interspersed with private lands. (See map on next page.) Users of the monument should take care not to infringe on private property rights.

Pilot Rock is probably the most prominent element of the monument. It is highly visible as one approaches the Siskiyous either from the north or south, and of course that is how the rock got its name. The Pacific Crest Trail runs close to the base of the rock, and some energetic souls climb it, although it is no pushover. There have even been two deaths, as a result of falls.

To get to Pilot Rock, leave I-5 at Exit 6, for Mount Ashland. Take Old Highway 99 to the south, bypass the Mount Ashland Road at 0.9 mile, go under the freeway, continue 1.2 miles beyond Mount Ashland Road, and turn left on Pilot Rock Road (gravel). At 2.0 miles on Pilot Rock Road there is a fork in the road; go right. A small parking lot lies 0.8 mile further, on the crest. The **Pacific Crest Trail** (PCT) goes along the crest.

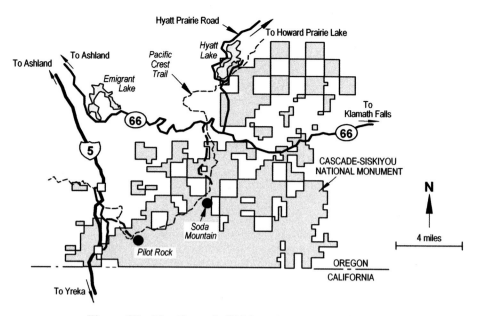

Figure 29 - The Cascade-Siskiyou National Monument

Another access to the PCT is provided by **Soda Mountain Road.** To get there, leave I-5 at Exit 14, and take OR 66 to the east for 14.6 miles. Soda Mountain road, (gravel), is on the right. Much of the land along the road is privately owned, so property rights should be respected. Drive slowly. At 3.7 miles, a power line goes over the road, and the Pacific Crest Trail crosses at this point. There is enough parking along the sides of the road for a few cars, and many people park here to take day hikes on the PCT, in both directions.

The southeast portion of **Hyatt Lake,** with campgrounds, and a little piece of the western shore are included in the national monument. These areas receive by far the most public use of the monument lands. In one location on the western shore, a nicely-developed wildlife watching site, with picnic tables and a restroom, has been constructed by BLM. Ospreys can usually be seen from here, plus an occasional bald eagle.

A feature of Hyatt Lake that some people find objectionable is the dead trees that were left behind when the reservoir was constructed. They stick up in the water like so many telephone poles. However, cormorants apparently think these were put there expressly for their benefit, and at times it seems as if most of the trees have cormorants perched on them. People sometimes are surprised to find cormorants at an inland location like this, because cormorants are supposed to be at the seashore. But this particular species -- the double-crested cormorant -- loves fresh water even more than salt water, and is found coast to coast at inland locations, as well as at the coast.

Crater Lake National Park

Crater Lake is a place of great beauty, and people come thousands of miles to see it. It has been called "Southern Oregon's Crown Jewel." Mostly, they come to the rim, gaze at the magnificent lake in wonder, and perhaps stop at a few other rim points to admire it. They might even hike down the trail to **Cleetwood Cove** and take a boat trip.

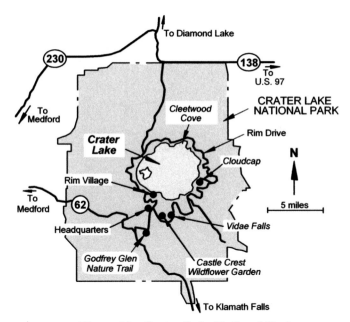

Figure 30 - Crater Lake National Park

Rim Village is the main point of activity, and attracts the crowds. A paved path leads along the edge of the rim, and some of the birds that visitors can hardly escape noticing are the ever-present Clark's nutcrackers. Nutcrackers are gray, black, and white birds that love high elevations. At the rim they fly from tree to tree, sounding their raucous calls, and seeking handouts and leftovers from the tourists.

The view of the magnificent lake from the rim is certainly the major reason for making the trip to Crater Lake, but the mountain has additional rewards that come with a closer acquaintance. For one thing, it is indeed a *mountain*, a big one that rises almost into alpine territory, although it happens to be missing its top. The high point of the rim road, at **Cloudcap** (7960 feet), is the highest point you can reach anywhere in Oregon by paved road, and the mountain has meadows and wildflowers and subalpine scenery that match the best anywhere.

A popular stop on the rim road is **Castle Crest Wildflower Garden**, about a mile from Park Headquarters. The trail through the "wildflower garden" is about a ¼-mile long, and requires some boulder-hopping. Much of it is situated on a steep slope below Castle Crest (hence, the name), and it is blessed with a number of springs. The roster of wildflower species in late July is impressive, including Lewis monkeyflowers, yellow monkeyflowers, wandering daisies, white bog-orchids, elephant heads, forget-me-nots, bleeding hearts, monkshood, and blue lupine.

The national park has many lovely spots, but one of the loveliest is **Godfrey Glen Nature Trail,** which is located about 1.4 miles from the entrance station, as you enter from the south. The trail is barrier-free, gently graded, and passes through a wonderful hemlock/fir forest. The stellar attraction is the view of Godfrey Glen, a meadow tucked into the bottom of the canyon below, surrounded by vertical cliffs and pinnacles. Barriers are provided at the best view sites. Since the cliffs are capped with loose ash, anyone approaching the edge could slip over those vertical walls with ease -- a warning for those with children. Stay on the trail.

Mount Ashland

In July, many residents of the warm Rogue Valley may not realize that they live within a short distance of a cool subalpine paradise. Behind **Mount Ashland**, the road runs for 13 miles at the 6000 to 7000-foot level, often rising into wonderful green meadows bordered by clumps of fir, and strewn with wildflowers.

The full route, from I-5 to Jacksonville, is 55 miles, with 23 miles of dusty road. Early July is the time to go, because before that the road is closed by snow. The departure point is Exit 6 from I-5, south of Ashland, where the sign says, "Mount Ashland." Follow the paved road to the Mount Ashland Ski Area.

The pavement ends after 9 miles, at the ski area. The next 13 miles are narrow and often one-way, but negotiable by an ordinary car in good weather. The Forest Service designates it as Road 20. Along the way, there are some sensational views of Mount Shasta toward the south. In July, wildflowers are profuse along the slopes next to the road.

At 10.2 miles, the road to the top of **Mount Ashland** branches off. It is 1.2 miles to the top of the mountain, along a rough one-way road that many people will decide to pass up. A high-clearance vehicle is desirable. The top of the mountain has tall antennas, a radar dome, and a ski lift. The view is sensational, with Mount McLoughlin to the north, and Mount Shasta to the south.

Continuing on Road 20, the wonderful meadows of **Grouse Gap** soon come into view, and the road to the Grouse Gap Shelter (restrooms) is encountered at 11.1 miles, measured from I-5. Grouse Gap Shelter is an attractive structure, and people often leave their cars here while they day-hike on the PCT.

From Grouse Gap, the road continues west, sometimes rough and narrow, to **Jackson Gap** (22.2 miles from I-5). Jackson Gap, at 7,061 feet, is the high point on the road. From here, a rough narrow road leads 2 miles to the top of **Dutchman Peak,** where there is a look-out. From the gap, Road 20 goes downhill, and leads ultimately to Ruch and Jacksonville.

Wildlife

Since the Rogue Valley is surrounded by mountains and forests, it seems reasonable that there should be lots of wild animals nearby. And so there are. Birds are probably the most visible animals, and the region abounds in bird life. The mammals are here, too, but usually are more secretive in behavior. A few of the larger ones are elk, deer, coyotes, black bears, and mountain lions. Mammals that are rumored to be present are wolverines and lynxes.

According to the Oregon Department of Fish and Wildlife, there are about 5,000 mountain lions in Oregon, and the area of the southwestern Cascades is one with high density. There have been no human deaths in Oregon because of mountain lion attacks, although there have been some in California. There is one record of an attack on a 10-year old boy near Junction City in 1972 by a young mountain lion, in which the boy was bitten and scratched.

The Department of Fish and Wildlife says that mountain lions usually avoid humans, but in the event you encounter one, the department says you should stay calm, maintain direct eye contact, and pick up children, but without bending down or turning your back. Do not run. Back away slowly, speaking loudly and firmly. Raise your arms and clap your hands. If attacked, the department says you should fight back with rocks, sticks, or anything available.

The species of bear we have in Oregon is called American black bear, and individuals can weigh up to 500 pounds and more. Grizzly bears can be twice as large, but today there are no grizzlies in Oregon, the last one having been killed in the late 1930s, in the northeastern part of the state. (However, there are grizzlies in Washington and Idaho.) Even though our bears are called "black" bears, they can sometimes be light brown to dark brown. Oregon is one of the states with a large population, estimated at 25,000 bears (1995). Even though bears are potentially dangerous, and contact should be avoided, there are no records of human deaths in Oregon resulting from bear attacks.

Elk are the largest mammals in our area, and can weigh as much as 1100 pounds. Even though they are regularly hunted, their population in Southwestern Oregon is believed to be healthy and increasing. On the other hand, deer in Western Oregon (specifically, black-tailed deer, a subspe-

Figure 31 - Siskiyou Crest beyond Mount Ashland

cies of mule deer), may be undergoing a population decline, partly because of habitat loss. Researchers claim that deer don't do well in dense mature forests because of scarcity of food, and prefer to feed on the deciduous shrubs and soft-stemmed plants that come in after a forest fire or clearcut.

There are no wolves in southwestern Oregon (except in zoos, of course), although it is reported that a few have crossed into northeastern Oregon from Idaho. Coyotes, on the other hand, are common. Canada lynx has been reported in Oregon. However, since they are highly secretive, you are unlikely to see one. Bobcats, on the other hand, are common, and often seen. Sometimes, large bobcats are reported as mountain lions. Wolverines formerly occurred in Oregon, and some think they still do, but their presence is not confirmed.

Figure 33 - Downtown Jacksonville

7 Jacksonville

"The Largest City in the State"

Jacksonville, originally known as Table Rock City, was the first city in Southern Oregon. It became the county seat of Jackson County in 1853, and by 1859 had become the largest city in the state. As originally established, Jackson County was enormous, and included lands which now lie in Coos, Curry, Josephine, Klamath, and Lake Counties.

Gold was discovered in 1851 in **Rich Gulch,** a branch of Daisy Creek, at a location on Applegate Street about three blocks south of downtown Jacksonville. There is a marker at the site, about 100 yards south of the junction of Applegate Street and Oregon Street. Later, the upper portion of Rich Gulch was the scene of some of the heaviest mining activity in the region. Initially the mining was by "panning," and then by means of sluices.

Figure 32 - OPPOSITE PAGE - Former Jackson County Court House, now the Jacksonville Museum.

By the 1870s hydraulic mining took over, using water from a mile-long ditch reaching to Jackson Creek, plus "back-up" water via a ditch from Poorman Creek, 7 miles away. The water was delivered through a high-pressure nozzle called a "Giant," from a holding reservoir located above the mining site. The high velocity jet of water excavated away the soil, permitting access to the gold. Because sufficient water is not available in the summer, the mining was done in winter. Mining continued until about 1940.

The area is accessible by the trail system of the **Jacksonville Woodlands Historic Natural Park and Trail System**. (See Page 64.) The evidence of hydraulic mining is plainly visible in upper Rich Gulch, but is being healed over by the growth of trees. Look out for poison oak, which is abundant.

Miners swarmed into the region after the discovery of gold, and in a short time Jacksonville had many thriving businesses. However, as with virtually all gold towns on the West Coast at that time, there were frequent fires, because most of the buildings were of wood. Between 1873 and 1884 there were three fires, and the result was that a city ordinance was passed requiring new construction to be of brick.

Other strikes were being made in the region. At Sterling Creek, about 7 miles south of Jacksonville, gold was found in 1854. In 1877 a ditch 26 miles long, called Sterling Ditch, was constructed to bring water from the upper Little Applegate River to Sterling Creek for hydraulic mining purposes, which continued until the 1930s. A thriving town called **Sterlingville**, with a population of 1200 at its peak, came into existence near the creek, and mining tailings are visible in the creek bed. Today, nothing remains of the town but Sterlingville Cemetery, situated about ¼ mile north of the intersection of Sterling Creek Road and Griffin Road. Another thing that remains is the Sterling Ditch itself, and the Bureau of Land Management maintains the **Sterling Mine Ditch Trail**, which runs along the ditch, for recreational purposes.

When the railroad bypassed Jacksonville in 1884 (see next page), the economy slowed. An unexpected benefit of this slowing was that many of the city's historical structures remained intact. In 1966, much of the city was declared to be a **National Historic Landmark**, covering about 100 buildings.

When the "great train robbery" took place in 1923 (see Page 39), the courthouse in Jacksonville was where the trial was held. It had taken four years for the robbers, the D'Autremont brothers, to be caught, so the trial was in 1927. For a time, Jacksonville was in the national news, because of the sensational nature of the crime. But, at about the same time, Jacksonville lost the county seat to its growing neighbor, Medford. The courthouse, vacant for 20 years, became a museum for the Southern Oregon Historical Society.

Another name associated with Jacksonville is that of Vance Colvig, born there in 1892. The name "Vance Colvig" might not ring a bell, but he was the one who later became Bozo the Clown. He also was the voice for "Grumpy," in Walt Disney's *Snow White and the Seven Dwarfs*, and for "Goofy," in many Walt Disney cartoons.

Today, the city is a prime tourist destination, and is also regarded by many as a highly attractive place to live. There are large expensive homes spotted about here and there, often in what seem to be fairly remote locations. The city sponsors numerous celebrations and events each year, such as a "Victorian Christmas" in December, and a Chinese New Year parade in February.

The Matter of the Railroad

Jacksonville had a stage line by 1860, and got a telegraph connection in 1864. But it wanted a railroad. As recounted in the previous chapter, construction on the railroad began in 1870, and by 1883 it reached the Rogue Valley. But it bypassed Jacksonville. Probably, the most influential factor was that a route through Medford would be on a reasonably straight line through the valley, whereas routing through Jacksonville would be longer, and involve steeper grades.

There was another factor. It developed that some land in the center of the valley was owned by a small group of men, including Cornelius Beekman, a leading banker in Jacksonville. They platted a town site, and donated land to the railroad for a station and switching yards, plus 41 city blocks in the new town. This became Medford.

The citizens of Jacksonville finally got their railroad, a branch line to Medford, by creating it themselves. It was affectionately known as the "Jacksonville Cannonball," and operated for 35 years. (See Page 41).

The Chinese

In the 1850s Chinese flocked to Jacksonville, mostly living together in shacks along Main Street, and taking menial jobs. (Main Street runs parallel to California Street, which is today's main street.) They encountered discriminatory laws, which prevented them from becoming citizens, from filing claims, or owning property. In many cases, they took to gleaning through mined areas that were considered "played out," to find small amounts of gold that had been left behind.

The Chinese were hard-working and kept to themselves, which probably contributed to them being disliked, or even feared. One expression of this was the provision, in the Oregon Constitution of 1859, that stated, "No Chinaman, not a resident of this State at the time of adoption of this Constitution, shall ever hold any real estate or mining claim, or work any mining claim therein." An additional expression of prejudice was the passage of The Chinese Exclusion Act in 1882 by the U.S. Congress, which made it unlawful for further Chinese immigration to the United States.

The constitutional ban on ownership of real estate or mining claims by Chinese, reportedly was widely ignored. A Chinese miner by the name of Gin Lin purchased mining claims in the Applegate Valley, and conducted extensive hydraulic mining operations there during the 1880s. He is said to have deposited over a million dollars of gold dust in a Jacksonville bank, which aroused resentment among other miners in the area. He returned to China in 1894. The National Forest Service has constructed a trail, called the "Gin Lin Mining Trail," through the hydraulically mined area.

Tunneling Under the Streets

In the 1920s, and especially during the depression years of the 1930s, there was a resurgence of gold mining in Jacksonville, of the backyard variety. Most found little gold, but some were able to find enough to buy groceries. A few went further. They began to build tunnels that sometimes reached beyond their own property lines, under other peoples' properties and under city streets. With the beginning of World War II, the incentive for backyard mining

Figure 34 - Collapsed street, as a result of tunneling. One wheel of a fire truck fell through, as shown in first photo. Second photo shows hole in pavement.
(Photos courtesy of Jacksonville Public Works Department.)

disappeared. However, in later years problems occasionally developed, such as when a tunnel that had been dug under a street collapsed under the weight of a passing vehicle.

Southern Oregon Historical Society

The Historical Society was formed in 1946. It operates several major historical sites, mostly in Jacksonville, including an **Historical Research Library** on Central Avenue in downtown Medford. The Society preserves collections of artifacts, offers educational programs for children, presents exhibitions, and manages the following sites:

Jacksonville Museum. The museum is in the former Jackson County Courthouse, on N. 5th Street, constructed in 1883. Exhibits include artifacts and photographs. Open Wednesdays through Sundays. (Entrance fee, which includes entry to the Children's Museum next door.)

Jacksonville Children's Museum. The museum is in the former jail house. Some of the exhibits are "hands-on", and include a pioneer cabin, a Native American lodge, a puppet theater, a general store, and a barber shop. The building also houses the History Store, with books, memorabilia, and toys. (Entrance fee includes entry to Jacksonville Museum, next door.)

Historic Hanley Farm. The 37-acre farm is on Hanley Road, between Jacksonville and Central Point. Members of the Hanley family lived on the farm until 1985, when it was bequeathed to the Historical Society. The smaller of the two barns was built in the 1850s, while the larger one was built in the 1900s. The farmhouse was built in the 1870s, and is a splendid example of the period. It, and other parts of the farm, are open for visitation on what are called the "First Weekends," namely, the first Saturdays and Sundays of June, July, August, and September. (Entrance fee charged. The farm can also be rented, for special events such as summer weddings and parties.)

C.C. Beekman House. Cornelius C. Beekman arrived in Jacksonville in 1853. Ten years later, he became a Wells Fargo agent, and opened his own bank in town. The house, at 420 E. California Street, is open for tours on the first weekends of each month in June, July, August, and September. (Entrance fee.) Behind the Beekman House is the delightful **Beekman Native Plant Arboretum,** open to the public. There is a one-mile loop trail (occasionally steep) above the arboretum, called the **Beekman Loop Trail**. The trail is a part of the Jacksonville Trail System (see next page).

The **C.C. Beekman Bank**, at 3rd and California Streets, downtown, is not open for tours, but has a "viewing alcove."

The U.S. Hotel. The hotel is a highly visible component of historical Jacksonville, right on the main street. It was constructed in the 1880s. President Rutherford B. Hayes and his wife stayed there in 1880. (Not open for tours, but can be rented for special events.)

Figure 35 - Historic house at Hanley Farms, dating from the 1870s.

Britt Festivals

Peter Britt arrived in Jacksonville in 1852, allegedly with only five dollars in his pocket. Initially, he tried mining gold, but soon turned to other activities, including running a mule pack train, planting orchards and wine grapes, and investing. Today, he is best known for the photographs he took over a period of many years. Many of his historical photographs are on display at the Jacksonville Museum.

His first dwelling was a log cabin on the site he claimed under the Donation Land Act, which today is the wonderful **Britt Gardens.** He was successful enough that he converted his cabin to a storage shed and constructed a house, which he periodically enlarged. By 1883, the house had spacious living quarters, a wine cellar, and two studios. The gardens contained horticultural specimens from all over the world, including a giant sequoia tree (native to the Sierra Nevada mountains of California) planted in 1862. Today, the **Britt Sequoia** is over 200 feet tall, has a circumference of 18 feet, and is listed as an Oregon Heritage Tree.

The house was destroyed by fire in 1960. The estate went to the Oregon University System, with the proviso that the grounds would be cared for. The property was subsequently bought by Jackson County, to be operated as a county park. The Britt Gardens are near the junction of West Pine Street and 1st Street. Parking is difficult in the area

The **Britt Festival** is one of the signature events of Southern Oregon. (It is officially referred to as the "Britt Festivals," in the plural, because the concerts are offered in two locations -- at the Britt Pavilion in Jacksonville, and at the Lithia Motors Ampitheater in Central Point.) The festivals began in 1963 at the Jacksonville location, with classical music only. The audience sat on the grass lawn in front of the stage. Bench seats were added in 1987, although many people continue to sit on the lawn behind the seats during performances. The current capacity is 2,200, with 662 of them reserved bench seats. The repertoire has been expanded beyond classical, to include dance, jazz, blues, folk, bluegrass, pop, and country, and includes world-class artists. Since it is outdoors, it operates in the summer months only. Some of the events are scheduled in the **Lithia Motors Ampitheater** located at the Jackson County Fairgrounds, because it is larger, with a capacity of 5,900.

Jacksonville Woodlands Historic Natural Park and Trail System.

The **Jacksonville Woodlands Association,** a non-profit organization, was founded in 1989, with the purpose of preserving forested open space in the Jacksonville area, and making it accessible by a system of trails. Its first project was to preserve the 21-acre Beekman Woods, which surrounds the historic Beekman House. The project was successful when the land was purchased by the City of Jacksonville. Today, the trail system has 15 hiking trails of varying difficulties, on lands owned by the City of Jacksonville, Jackson County, or the Bureau of Land Management, a total of 310 acres. A trail map can be obtained from the **Jacksonville Woodlands Association,** Box 1210, Jacksonville, OR 97530, or at its website at www.jvwoodlands.org.

A trail of special interest is the **Sarah Zigler Interpetive Trail, a** 2-mile loop, relatively flat, beginning and ending in the historic Britt Gardens, that has been designated as a National Recreation Trail. It leads along Jackson Creek to the 1851 gold discovery site. However, this was not the discovery that set off the big rush, which was one made a little later in Rich Gulch. Also, see **Beekman Loop Trail,** above, which lies behind the C.C. Beekman House.

The Jacksonville Woodlands Association has no paid staff, is entirely volunteer, and is managed by an 11-member Board of Directors.

A Botanical Celebrity

In 1999, Jacksonville discovered it had a local celebrity -- a beautiful wild lily called Gentner's Fritillary (*Fritillaria gentneri*), which had just been officially declared to be Federally Endangered. The lily had first been discovered in 1944 by members of the Gentner family, on a hillside near Jacksonville. (The "G" in Gentner is pronounced as in "good," rather than with a "j" sound.) In later years, the lily has been declared to be "one of the rarest native plants in the world," with small groups of plants growing in Jackson and Josephine counties, plus a few growing just barely over the California border. About three-quarters of the plants grow within a 7-mile radius of Jacksonville. In the spring of 2005, the Jacksonville Chamber of Commerce created an annual **"Fritillary Festival"** in its honor.

Figure 36 - Gentner's Fritillary

The flowers are large and usually "ox-blood" red (see photo), as contrasted with the brighter scarlet color of a more common relative, the Scarlet Fritillary. Also, the petals are not as sharply turned back ("recurved") as they are with Scarlet Fritillary. The risks to the plant are caused by such things as trail and road construction, housing developments, predation by wildlife, and, sadly, people who dig up the bulbs, perhaps just because they are known to be endangered. (Digging them up, of course, is illegal, because the plants are federally protected.)

Jacksonville Inn

The Jacksonville Inn is one of the most highly visible structures in Jacksonville, It was constructed in 1861, and is listed in the National Historic Register. It has eight hotel rooms for rent, and three "honeymoon cottages" a couple of blocks away. Its restaurant has been recognized by the Pacific Northwest Magazine as one of Oregon's best restaurants, and it claims to have a wine list of more than 2,000 wines. President George W. Bush and Laura Bush stayed in one of the cottages, while campaigning in Oregon.

The Applegate Valley

The Applegate River is a major tributary of the Rogue River, and joins the Rogue near Grants Pass. Applegate Road traverses the upper valley, and OR 238 traverses most of the lower valley. Several small communities, Ruch (pronounced "Roosh"), Applegate, and Murphy, are along OR 238. Williams is about 5 miles south of OR 238. Many people simply refer to the valley as "The Applegate."

Applegate Lake, about 15 miles south of Ruch, extends almost to the border with California. The lake is nearly 5 miles long, is popular for boating and fishing, and has campgrounds, picnic areas, and three boat ramps. The dam that created the lake was constructed by the U.S. Army Corps of Engineers, primarily for flood control purposes, and was completed in 1980.

Figure 37 - The post office at Buncom

Buncom

Buncom is a delightful little "vest pocket" ghost town, with just three old buildings: a bunkhouse, a cookhouse, and a post office. (For another Oregon ghost town, see page 94.) To get there, turn onto Applegate Road from Highway 234 at Ruch. Go 2.8 miles to Little Applegate Road, turn left, and go 2.9 miles to Buncom, at the intersection of Little Applegate Road and Sterling Creek Road.

Buncom got its start because of the gold mining on nearby Sterling Creek. For a time, it served as a supply center for the Little Applegate Valley, but as the gold diminished and autos increased, Buncom went into decline. During the Depression, squatters reportedly lived in the buildings. In the 1990s, the Buncom Historical Society was established to preserve the site. Each year, the society sponsors **Buncom Day** on Memorial Day weekend, with live music, craft and food booths, and what the society calls **The World-Famous Buncom Chicken-Splat Contest.** In the contest, the floor of a chicken cage is divided into numbered squares, and people can select a square for 25 cents each. At the end of the day, a chicken is placed in the cage. When it "splats," those who picked the winning square get the money.

Figure 39 - The Plaza

8 Ashland

"A Special Place"

Chances are, if you were taking a word-association test and the word "Ashland" was mentioned, the first word to come to mind would be "Shakespeare." Because of this, the name "Ashland" has more recognition outside the state than do its larger neighbors, Medford and Grants Pass. There are people in other states who regard an annual trip to Ashland for Shakespeare to be one of the essentials of life.

But Ashland is much more. Its downtown section is renowned for its attractiveness, and its "strollability." In 2000, the downtown district, including the Plaza, was listed on the National Register of Historic Places. Visitors from England are often struck by how much the downtown reminds them of small cities in the British Isles. In addition, Ashland is the "sister city" of **Guanajuato, Mexico,** and one of its most attractive spots is a sidewalk called

Figure 38 - OPPOSITE PAGE - The Elizabethan Stage.

Guanajuato Way (Calle Guanajuato), which runs along the edge of the creek behind the shops on the Plaza. The sidewalk is lined with tables and umbrellas, and the creekside dining is about as nice an experience as you can find anywhere. In 2006, Money Magazine selected Ashland as one of the best places in America to retire.

Among the many regular events in Ashland are: the **Rogue Valley Growers and Crafters Market,** Tuesday mornings at the Armory, March through November; a **Fourth of July Celebration,** with a parade in the morning downtown, and music in Lithia Park in the afternoon; and the **Old Ashland Walking Tour,** held Monday-Saturday from mid-June to mid-September (meet at the information booth in the Plaza a little before 10:00 a.m.)

One of Ashland's better-known personalities is Ann Curry, the NBC news anchor on the "Today" show, who grew up in Ashland. She graduated from the University of Oregon, and got her start in news work at KTVL in Medford.

Ashland had its beginning in 1852, at the location where the Plaza is located today, with a flour mill. At that time, it was known as Ashland Mills. It rapidly became one of the major settlements in the Rogue Valley, contesting with Jacksonville for prominence. But Jacksonville had the gold, so Ashland lost that contest. But today, in the 21st century, the roles of the two cities are reversed, and Ashland won the contest after all. Something that played a part in its rise was a thing called "Chautauqua."

Chautauqua

The name "Chatauqua" was one to reckon with at about the end of the 19th century, when it brought a broad education and entertainment program to communities nationwide. It began in 1872 with religious and Bible study, but then expanded to include teachers, lecturers, explorers, politicians, orchestras, concert bands, stage plays, opera singers, jugglers, and magicians. It mostly ended its popularity in the late 1920s, because of the advent of autos, radios, and movies. However, it is still active today at its original site at Lake Chautauqua in New York State, and there is even an Oregon Chautauqua, sponsored by the Oregon Council for the Humanities.

In Ashland, the Oregon Shakespeare Festival can trace its history back to the Chautauqua. Many of the Chautauqua activities across the country were held in huge tents, but in Ashland the citizens built a Chautauqua building in 1893, on the hill above the Plaza, and then enlarged it in 1917. After the decline in popularity of the movement in the 1920s, the Ashland building was torn down, and only the foundations remained.

Oregon Shakespeare Festival

The old Chautauqua foundation provided the inspiration to Angus Bowmer, of Southern Oregon Normal School (now Southern Oregon University), to use it in presenting two Shakespeare plays, in 1935. In 1959, the present outdoor theater was constructed within the cement walls of the original Chautauqua. Today, the outdoor **Elizabethan Stage** has 1200 seats, and two indoor theaters have been added -- the **Angus Bowmer** Theater (600 seats), and **the New Theater** (350 seats).

The extensive repertoire not only includes Shakespearean plays, but also many contemporary works, which are offered from February through October. The outdoor theater operates from June to the beginning of October, and during this period the free **Green Show**, featuring music and dance, is offered each evening in front of the outdoor theater. The Oregon Shakespeare Festival is patronized by 120,000 customers per year.

Ashland Springs Hotel

The 9-story hotel is the most visible feature in downtown Ashland. It was built in 1925, and was first known as the **Lithia Springs Hotel**, but failed to capture the expected business. In 1961, it was re-named the **Mark Antony Hotel,** to try to capitalize on the Shakespeare Festival. When that failed to improve the hotel's fortunes, it was purchased by a new owner, who undertook an extensive restoration, and re-named it the **Ashland Springs Hotel.** Whatever the name, it is the pre-eminent Ashland landmark. In 1978, it was placed on the National Register of Historic Places.

Oregon Cabaret Theatre

The Oregon Cabaret Theatre began in 1986 in Ashland's old First Baptist Church. The church was originally built in 1911, but had been owned by several different people, and finally had become vacant. Along the way, someone had painted it pink, and it was known as "The Old Pink Church." Beginning in 1982, the old church was restored to its 1911 appearance, and was reborn as the Cabaret Theatre.

The theater has 140 seats, and offers six shows a week year-round, of musicals, revues, and comedies. The owners say that the shows are "presented in an elegant nightclub setting," with seating either on the main floor or in the balcony. You may, if you choose, have dinner before the show, although that requires advance reservations. Or, if you prefer, you may just have appetizers and drinks.

Rogue Valley Symphony

The symphony is affiliated with Southern Oregon University (SOU), and has been serving the Rogue Valley since 1967. Classical concerts are given at three locations during the season. These are: the SOU music recital hall, located in the Music Building on Mountain Avenue in Ashland; the Craterian Ginger Rogers Theater in downtown Medford (see page 78); and the Grants Pass High School Performing Arts Center, on NE 9th Street in Grants Pass.

Southern Oregon University

Not only is Ashland the home of the Oregon Shakespeare Festival, it is also a college town, because of **Southern Oregon University (SOU),** a wonderful regional asset with programs ranging from theater arts to science to business and beyond. It has been designated a Center of Excellence in the Fine and Performing Arts by the Oregon University System, with a new 11-million dollar **Center for the Visual Arts,** and **Schneider Museum of Art.**

In 2006, the *New York Times* published an article entitled "Off the Beaten Path," listing 20 colleges that were considered to be **"hidden gems,"** that stress undergraduate teaching, and have achieved strong scholarship levels. SOU was one of them, singled out primarily because of its theater arts program, its connection to the Oregon Shakespeare Festival, and an "exceptional English and liberal arts curriculum." The article added, ". . . the festival and university

Figure 40 - On the campus of Southern Oregon University

seem to thrive, thanks to mountainous surroundings that attract tourists and faculty." Other colleges in the West that were listed are: Pitzer College, in Claremont, Califonia; Santa Clara University, in Santa Clara, California; Mills College, in Oakland, California; Evergreen State College, in Olympia, Washington; Whitman College, in Walla Walla, Washington; and Colorado College, in Colorado Springs, Colorado.

The University is more than theater arts, of course. It has almost 5,000 students, with over 35 majors and 100 academic programs, including programs as diverse as art, biology, business, chemistry, computer science, criminology, economics, education, English, environmental studies, geography, geology, history, international studies, psychology, mathematics, music, Native American studies, nursing, philosophy, physics, political science, sociology, theater arts, and women's studies. At the graduate level, SOU has Master's programs in computer science, education, environmental education, management, applied psychology, and music.

The University offers night and weekend classes at its **Medford Campus** in business, communication, computer science, criminology, education, human service, military science, psychology, and sociology. Beginning in 2005, it began offering **Distance Learning** programs, online, in business, and criminology and criminal justice.

SOU has undergone many name changes. Its roots go back as far as 1869, when it was set up as a church-sponsored school that later became Southern Oregon Normal School. In 1956 it was re-named Southern Oregon College (SOC), and in 1975 Southern Oregon State College (SOSC). Some people still refer to it as SOC (pronounced "sock") or as SOSC (pronounced "sosk"). In 1997 it became Southern Oregon University.

In **intercollegiate athletics,** SOU teams (calling themselves the "Raiders") compete in the NAIA (National Association of Intercollegiate Athletics), a small-college alternative to the National Collegiate Athletic Association (NCAA). Men's and women's sports are sponsored in basketball, track and field, and cross country. Men's sports are sponsored in football and wrestling, and women's sports are sponsored in volleyball, tennis, softball, and soccer.

Figure 41 - In Lithia Park

Lithia Park

Lithia Park is a marvelous woodland park tucked into the edge of Ashland, with a mountain stream, hiking trails, rhododendrons, azaleas, Japanese garden, playgrounds, and band shell. To some, it looks like a miniature version of the famous Golden Gate Park in San Francisco. And no wonder, because John McLaren, superintendent of Golden Gate Park, had a hand in the development of Lithia Park. Not all of McLaren's ideas were used. For example, he envisioned that the park would include a mineral springs resort, with a sanitarium. This part of the plan did not take place. Instead, Lithia Park became a "passive park in a wilderness setting."

The park, in one form or another, has a 150-year history. In the early Chautauqua days, people came by railroad and by wagon, and many of them set up their tents along Ashland Creek, below the Chautauqua building. Gradually, a park came into being, owned by the

Figure 42 - Wood Duck in Lithia Park

Chautauqua Association, but open to the public. Proposals were made to create a city-owned park along the creek, and the people of Ashland, in 1908, voted to tax themselves for that purpose.

The old flour mill along the creek, which had fallen into disrepair and had become an eyesore, was removed. The grounds were landscaped, and paths were constructed. Lithia water was piped in to an artificially constructed cave known as "Satan's Sulphur Grotto." There was even a free auto camp near where the park office is located today.

Lithia Park, as beautiful and tranquil as it may seem, has not always been so peaceful. At least twice, once in 1974 and again in 1996, devastating floods have swept down the creek and through the Plaza, destroying bridges and creating havoc. Each time, the citizens of Ashland have rallied to reconstruct their beloved park, and today it shows little evidence of the floods.

The park begins next to the Plaza in downtown Ashland. A trail guide can be purchased at the park office, which describes a one-mile route that will take you on a circuit completely around the park. The trail guide will help you identify the trees and shrubs you see, which are both native and introduced. The **Japanese Garden** is a delight, especially in autumn, when it glows with color. The **Upper Duck Pond** is another special attraction, both for its landscaping, and for its resident wood ducks.

Ashland Creek runs the length of the park, and is the prototype of the perfect babbling mountain brook. American dippers (a species of bird, once called "water ouzel") are here, although most visitors overlook them. Each December, the Audubon Society conducts a "dipper walk" along the creek, usually turning up 5 to 7 dippers.

Lithia Water

In the Plaza downtown, there is a drinking fountain that supplies lithia water. The fountain is popular with tourists, but, together with the pipes that supply it, represents a constant maintenance problem for the city. The water contains lithium*, of course, but also has high amounts of sulfur, sodium, calcium, and chlorine. Many people ascribe curative powers to the mineralized water, but others merely think it has a bad odor and taste.

---

* As a technical matter, *lithium* is a metallic element; *lithia* is an oxide of lithium.

The water is brought by cast iron pipes from its source about four miles to the east, not far from the Ashland Airport. It is pumped from about 120 feet deep, and is naturally cool (in other words, not hot, as in a hot springs). There is a branch pipeline flowing to a gazebo in Lithia Park, where another drinking fountain is located.

The name "Lithia" is permanently wedded to the name "Ashland." Lithia Park, Lithia Way (a major downtown street), and numerous commercial establishments bearing the name are all found in Ashland. In the region, and even beyond, the name "Lithia" is frequently seen on automobile license plates. Lithia Motors, one of the largest employers in the Rogue Valley, got its start in a small store on Ashland's Plaza, in 1946. Today, headquartered in Medford, it has 94 stores and 186 franchises in 12 western states.

Jackson Hot Springs

Just north of Ashland are the Jackson Hot Springs, adjacent to Highway 99. These have been in operation since the 1860s, and thousands of people have come to "partake of the waters." The current operation carries the name "Jackson Wellsprings," and features a swimming pool with water coming from the hot springs. Nearby, is Lithia Springs Resort and Gardens, which features hot mineral water from artesian wells.

ScienceWorks Hands-On Museum

In 2002, ScienceWorks began operations in a building previously occupied by the Pacific Northwest Museum of Natural History. The museum has nearly 100 interactive exhibits that encourage children and adults to learn more about science. As of 2004, it had served over 50,000 visitors and 10,000 school children. It is located on East Main Street in Ashland, and is open Wednesdays through Sundays.

Forensics Laboratory

The **National Fish and Wildlife Forensics Laboratory,** on East Main Street in Ashland, is an unusual laboratory indeed. In fact, it is the only one like it in the world. Its purpose is to support law enforcement officers in examining physical evidence relating to violation of wildlife laws. The kinds of things the lab might be sent, to examine, are blood samples, tissue samples, bones, teeth, hair, hides, feathers, and stomach contents, among others. An important matter the lab has to determine is if the death of an animal occurred because of another animal, or because of a violation of law. Tours by members of the public are not available, partly because of the severe guidelines on the handling of evidence that might be used in a court case.

A natural question is, why did the lab get located in Ashland? To this, the lab personnel sometimes respond with, "Why not?" One factor was that the State of Oregon offered four acres of free land, and provided funds for paving the access road and for utility lines. Lab personnel point out that six other potential sites were researched in detail, and Ashland was the winner.

Klamath Bird Observatory

Since the Klamath Bird Observatory (KBO) is located in Ashland, people often ask, "Why is the word 'Klamath' in the name?" The answer is that the word "Klamath" best describes the region in which KBO does its work. It has its headquarters in Ashland, partly because Ashland is centrally located in the region of its operations, and because it is a desirable place to live. Also, since one of its partners is Southern Oregon University, the location is appropriate. KBO's headquarters are on East Main Street, but it also operates out of the Upper Klamath Lake Field Station at Rocky Point, Oregon, and the Humboldt Bay Bird Observatory in Arcata, California.

KBO conducts scientific studies to monitor bird populations in the Klamath-Siskiyou Bioregion of Southern Oregon and Northern California, and maintains long term monitoring programs in the Rogue Valley at stations in Ashland, Medford, Grants Pass, and Cave Junction. Some of KBO's other research projects include: grazing and bird abundance; using birds to monitor the effects of fire; effects of water management on non-game birds; and effects of timber harvest practices on birds. Its educational program provides interpretation of the data for land managers and the public. Some of its partners are Boise Corporation, Bureau of Land Management, Bureau of Reclamation, Jackson County, Klamath County, National Park Service, Oregon Department of Fish and Wildlife, U.S. Fish and Wildlife Service, and U.S. Forest Service.

Figure 44 - Craterian Ginger Rogers Theater and Vogel Plaza

9 Medford

"The Middle Ford on Bear Creek"

The Agate Desert

The Agate "Desert," generally speaking, is that part of the Rogue Valley lying northeast of Central Point, where much of Medford's industrial development has taken place. During World War II, this is where Camp White was located. (See Page 80.) The residents of Jacksonville in the late 1800s, who were annoyed because the railroad had not come through their own city, generally referred to Medford as "Chaparral City," because of its location next to the Agate Desert. But it is not really a desert at all. Some of Southern Oregon's most beautiful wildflowers bloom there in spring, especially on The Nature Conservancy's **Agate Desert Preserve**, at the intersection of Table Rock and Antelope Roads. And Bear Creek passes right

---

Figure 43 - OPPOSITE PAGE - Bear Creek Park, Medford, in spring.

through the middle of the city, accompanied by the **Bear Creek Greenway** (see Page 99) with sections of it landscaped in lovely parks, such as **Bear Creek Park** in the south part of town.

The Agate Desert is a gravelly outwash plain, with a hard pan situated a foot or two below the surface. This configuration allows vernal pools to be created, and that, in turn, leads to special wildflower displays. Agates, which are a form of quartz, work their way to the surface, hence the name. Agates are found many places in Oregon, especially on ocean beaches.

Medford owes its location next to the Agate Desert to the decision by the railroad to locate a town along Bear Creek, and to establish a station there. (See Page 61, on the bypassing of Jacksonville by the railroad.) The original proposal for a name was "Middleford," because the middle ford of Bear Creek was nearby. Other suggestions were: East Jacksonville, Grand Central, and Phippsville. A railroad engineer, who was from Medford, Massachusetts, suggested that the name be "Medford," and that became its name. Perhaps "Medford" was also considered to be an abbreviation of "Middleford." Downtown Medford today contains a modern parking structure called Middleford Parking Facility, and an adjacent Middleford Alley.

For about 10 years, beginning in 1913, Medford had a trolley system. It ran on Main Street, from Oakdale to Keene Way. Later, the line was combined with the short line railroad that operated from Jacksonville to Medford (See Page 41), but operations ceased in 1924.

Medford is the economic center of Southern Oregon, and is its largest city by far. It is rapidly expanding, which causes some of its residents to be alarmed about traffic and congestion. It has a great variety of events, some of which are: the **Pear Blossom Festival,** in April, with arts and crafts exhibits, a parade, and a 10-km run; the **Rogue Valley Growers and Crafters Market**, Thursday mornings at the Armory, March through mid-November; **Downtown Market,** Saturday mornings, downtown, June through September; **Rogue Valley Balloon Rally**, July, at the Medford Airport; **Medford Jazz Jubilee**, October, at seven locations in Medford. Some other events and activities are described in the following sections.

Craterian Ginger Rogers Theater

The Craterian Ginger Rogers Theater and adjacent Vogel Plaza could be considered as the "center" of downtown Medford. The 750-seat theater presents performances in dance, music, musical theater, opera, ballet, symphony, comedy, and special events such as the **Miss Rogue Valley Scholarship Pageant,** a preliminary to the Miss America contest. Its "Art Partners", all of whom perform at the theater, are the **Rogue Opera, Rogue Valley Chorale, Rogue Valley Symphony, Ballet Rogue, Youth Symphony of Southern Oregon**, and the **Rogue Valley Youth Choruses.**

The theater was constructed in 1924, and originally hosted vaudeville acts and silent movies. A "naming contest" was conducted, with 1500 entries, and the name "Craterian Theater", in reference to nearby Crater Lake, was the winner. In 1926, just 18 months after the theater opened, Ginger Rogers danced on stage. She was 15 years old, and was participating in a six-month theater tour, as a result of having won a Charleston dance competition in Texas. In 1926 the theater received the first sound system between Sacramento and Portland, but by 1984, unable to compete with multiplexes, it closed.

Community efforts, plus an urban renewal program, brought it back to life again in 1998, as a "state of the art" performing arts facility, at a cost of 5 million dollars. At that time, it was given the name of "Craterian Ginger Rogers Theater."

Figure 45 - Model locomotive at Railroad Park

Ginger Rogers was a part-time resident of the Rogue Valley for 50 years, from 1940 to 1990. She owned a 1000-acre ranch on the Rogue River near Shady Cove, and lived there with her mother for many months each year. In 1982 she said, "I consider myself an Oregonian . . . I vote in Oregon and pay my taxes here." In 1993, as the campaign to revive the Craterian Theater was under way, she appeared on the stage in a personal interview, concluding with a showing of one of her movies.

She made 73 movies, and won an Academy Award for Best Actress in 1941, for her role in *Kitty Foyle.* For a time, she was the highest paid performer in Hollywood. She is best known for the ten movies she made with her dancing partner, Fred Astaire. It was said, "She did everything Fred Astaire did, and did it backwards and in high heels." (The quote has been attributed to Faith Whittlesey, former U.S. ambassador to Switzerland, and also to a *Frank and Ernest* cartoon.)

Railroad Park

Not only does this park have antique railroad cars to view, but you can also ride on miniature built-to-scale trains, on the second and fourth Sunday of each month from April through October. The rides are free and operated by volunteers, but they will be glad to accept your donations. The park is operated by the Southern Oregon Chapter of the National Railway

Historical Society, the Southern Oregon Live Steamers, the Morse Telegraph Club, and the Rogue Valley Model Railroad Club, all in cooperation with the Medford Parks and Recreation Department. In addition to the antique railroad cars and the free rides, there is a display of HO-scale model trains, and an antique telegraph system.

To get to the Railroad Park, go 0.2 mile north on Table Rock Road from Highway 99 to the intersection of Table Rock Road and Berrydale Avenue (signal). Turn right to the Railroad Park.

Rogue Valley Cup Soccer Tournament

The soccer tournament, held each May in Medford and Ashland, has been in existence since 1993, and is claimed to be the largest annual weekend event in Jackson County. About 200 teams attend, from California, Idaho, Nevada, Oregon, and Washington, with more than 3,000 players, both boys and girls, ranging from 10 through 19 years. It is said that almost 13,000 people are involved, including players, parents, siblings and spectators.

Who Was Roxy Ann?

Roxy Ann Peak, 3,571 feet in elevation. is highly visible from most parts of Medford. (Some have called it Roxy Ann Butte.) It is a Medford City Park, named **Prescott Park.** In the 1930s, the Civilian Conservation Corps (CCC) constructed trails, picnic areas, and scenic overlooks on the peak. There are roads leading to the summit, but the park does not allow public auto traffic, and sometimes it may be closed because of potential fire hazards. Most of the year, it is open to hiking and equestrian use.

There is some dispute over the naming of the peak. It has been stated that it was originally known as Skinner Butte, after an early settler. Another story is that it was named after Roxana Baker, another early resident. The accepted version is that it was named after Roxy Ann Bowen, who lived near the base of the peak in the 1850s.

The Black Bird

Grants Pass has its Caveman (see Page 89). Medford has its Black Bird. The Black Bird, 29 feet tall, made of plaster and papier-mâché, stands in a parking lot along West Main Street. It is the "mascot" of a sporting goods store that advertises it is open "8 days a week." One person claims that when she was little, she used to come from the next town just to see the bird, but another said, when he saw the bird the first time, he nearly ran off the road. At Christmas the Black Bird wears a Santa hat, and at Easter it has bunny ears. The owner of the sporting goods store says it may be one of the most photographed landmarks in Medford.

Camp White

Camp White existed from 1942 until 1947, during World War II, and was named for Major General George A. White of the Oregon National Guard. At its peak, it covered 77 square miles, housed 40,000 soldiers, and was the second largest "city" in Oregon, almost four times as big as Medford in 1941. The area chosen was the Agate Desert, because it was big, open, and relatively flat.

Besides the central core, there were two huge areas used for field training and maneuvers. One of them, known as the Beagle Range, was north of the Rogue River, near the intersection of OR 234 and Antioch Road. The other, known as the Antelope Range, extended east into the Antelope Valley. Concrete bunkers were constructed on the Beagle Range, to provide practice in taking enemy strongholds. Remnants of the old bunkers are still there. An imitation "Nazi village" was constructed on the Antelope Range, to provide practice in storming the mock town.

The peak of activity was in 1942-43, but by 1944 the camp operated on a much reduced scale. Part of it was used as a camp for 2000 prisoners of war. Most of the prisoners were young draftees, and many seemed to be relieved to be no longer in battle. Two prisoners escaped from the camp, but were apprehended the next day, still dressed in their prison garments, along the Lake of the Woods highway, claiming to be "headed for the middle west." Another pair, headed for Mexico, eluded capture for two weeks, but were finally apprehended near Crescent City.

Figure 46 - The Black Bird

After World War II, the base hospital became the core of the Veterans Administration Domiciliary, now known as **Southern Oregon Rehabilitation Center and Clinics.** A large portion of the acreage became the White City Industrial Park, some of it became White City, a portion was given to the State of Oregon to create Tou Velle State Park, a large portion became the Jackson County Sports Park, 1500 acres became the **Kenneth E. Denman Wildlife Refuge,** and the sewer treatment plant on Kirtland Road was transferred to the City of Medford.

White City today has almost 6000 people, and advertises itself as "A Great Place to Live." Though it is an unincorporated community, the residents have formed the White City Community Improvement Association. The business section extends along OR 62, and on Antelope Road. There is a post office, a supermarket, restaurants, and a number of other businesses. The civic center contains a sheriff's office, social service center, and a branch of the Jackson County Library.

Phoenix

Phoenix (calling itself "The Other Phoenix" -- a reference to Phoenix, Arizona) was one of the first towns established in the Rogue Valley, in 1851. Jacksonville soon passed it in population because of the gold strikes, but Phoenix remained important, and was one of the stops on the stage line when it came through. Medford, which is now many times larger, didn't appear until 30 years later, when the railroad put it on the map. Today, Phoenix has a population of about 4,500 people. As it grows, and as its neighbor, Medford, also grows, the boundary between the two becomes harder to distinguish.

The original name of the town was "Gasburg." The story is that there was a young woman named Kate in the town, who helped as a cook and waitress for the men who were employed at the lumber mill. Apparently, she was able to carry on several conversations at once, and still perform her duties of cooking and waiting on tables. Thus, she was given the name of "Gassy Kate" by her admirers, and when the matter of a name for the town came up, the vote was for "Gasburg."

"Gasburg" it was, for 20 years. Then, when a post office was established, the name "Phoenix" was chosen, because the building in which the post office was located also housed the office of the Phoenix Insurance Company. But it was a long time before the locals would give up their name of "Gasburg."

Eden Valley Orchards, on Voorhies Avenue between Medford and Phoenix, is listed in the National Register of Historic Places, and is said to be the "birthplace of the pear industry in Oregon." The **Rogue Valley Wine Center** is at the same location, and features wines from EdenVale and other regional wineries. The magnificent **Voorhies Mansion**, constructed in 1885, is the centerpiece of the property.

Talent

Talent, with a population of about 5,800, is somewhat larger than its neighbor, Phoenix. It got its start at about the same time as Phoenix, when Jacob Wagner settled there in 1852. A couple of years later, in connection with the Indian wars, the military established what was called "Fort Wagner."

It is said that the first name associated with the town was "Wagner Creek Fort," but others say it was simply "Wagner Creek," and still others say that the name of "Vernon" was proposed. Finally, the name "Talent" was selected, from Aaron P. Talent, who had established a retail business there, and had platted the townsite. Some well-known geographical features in the region are named for the first settler, Jacob Wagner, such as Wagner Creek, Wagner Butte, and Wagner Gap.

The community had a strong part to play in the early agricultural development of the Rogue Valley, and claims many "firsts" in the area, such as the first peach orchard, the first grapes grown, the first wheat and oats, and the first irrigation system.

Today, the irrigation system is extensive, operated by the **Talent Irrigation District (TID)**, headquartered in Talent. The district cooperates with the Medford Irrigation District and the Rogue River Valley Irrigation District through an organization known as Rogue Basin Water Users Council, Inc. Combined, the three systems serve about 35,000 acres in the Rogue Valley. The water supply of these districts comes partly from Bear Creek and Little

Butte Creek, but is augmented by about 30,000 acre-feet annually which is brought into the Rogue Basin from the Klamath River watershed on the east side of the Cascades. Water is also brought over the ridge from the west, via a canal that taps McDonald Creek, on the watershed of Little Applegate River. The canal, called "McDonald Ditch" passes through Wagner Gap, where the Wagner Creek Road (gravel) goes today.

TID's east-side water comes from Howard Prairie Lake and Hyatt Lake, through a tunnel under the Cascade crest, near Green Springs summit (see map on Page 51). Before those large reservoirs existed, a small dam was built on Keene Creek in 1924, a few miles below the present site of Hyatt Lake, creating what is known as **Little Hyatt Lake.** A canal from this dam carried water around the hill and over the divide, into Emigrant Lake in the Bear Creek Valley. It was operated until the 1950s, when Howard Prairie and Hyatt Lakes came into existence. When this happened, the canal over the divide was abandoned (remnants are still visible), but Little Hyatt Lake remained.

In 1998, the Bureau of Land Management recommended that the dam at Little Hyatt Lake be demolished. There was an outcry of protest among those who love the little lake created by the dam, and, as of this writing, Little Hyatt Lake is still there. To see it, take the Green Springs Highway (OR 66) from Ashland to the Green Springs summit, and turn left. It is about 3 miles, on gravel, to Little Hyatt Lake. The Pacific Crest Trail passes just below the dam.

Central Point

Central Point got its name because it was the intersection, in the center of the valley, of two important wagon roads. One was the road from the Willamette Valley to Sacramento, and the other was the road from Jacksonville to Sams Valley. With a population of about 16,000 in 2005, it is one of the fastest-growing areas in Jackson County. It is the "home city" of the Jackson County Fairground and Exposition Park. (See next section.)

Central Point also is the location of the **Crater Rock Museum**, an outstanding collection of fluorescent minerals, fossils, geodes, agates, petrified wood, dinosaur eggs, tropical shells, Native American artifacts, and more. Its mineral collection is world-class. The owner and operator is the Roxy Ann Gem and Mineral Society, and it's free (donations accepted). Open Tuesday through Saturday. Location: 2002 Scenic Ave., in Central Point, 0.4 mi. north of the intersection of Highway 99 and Scenic Ave.

Figure 47 - Fossil saber-tooth tiger skull at Crater Rock Museum.

Fairgrounds and Exposition Park

The fairgrounds in Central Point are used for many special events, such as the **Master Gardeners Spring Fair,** in April each year. But the major event is the **Jackson County Fair,** held the third weekend in July. The fair not only has the usual things that county fairs have, such as a carnival, local entertainment, livestock exhibits, quilt shows, and baked goods, but it also features major entertainers at the **Lithia Motors Amphitheater,** which has a capacity of 5900, with 1900 reserved seats, and 4000 "lawn spaces."

Another major event, held at the end of September each year, is the **Harvest Fair.** The sponsors of the fair say it ". . . celebrates the bounty of the harvest . . ." with product displays, livestock exhibits, crafts, and local microbrews and wines available for tasting. Contributing to the fun are such things as the "grape stomp," lawnmower races, and antique tractor pulls.

Southern Oregon Research and Extension Center

The Center, located on Hanley Road about four miles south of Central Point, is a partnership between Jackson County and Oregon State University. Its programs include 4-H, integrated pest management, wine grape production, family and community development, forest resource management, sustainability of small farms, livestock and forage research, and the master's gardener program.

The **J. Herbert Stone Nursery,** a part of the U.S. Forest Service, is near the Extension Center, on Old Stage Road. Its purpose is to grow seedlings for the Forest Service and other governmental agencies, for forest restoration.

Eagle Point

Eagle Point, ten miles north of Medford, got its name from a nearby roosting point for eagles. It calls itself "The Gateway to the Lakes." The population in 2006 was about 6,600. It is the home of the **Eagle Point National Cemetery**, but one of its best-known attractions is the Butte Creek Mill.

Butte Creek Mill, which is on the National Register of Historic Places, got its start in 1872, and derives its power from Little Butte Creek. Originally, it was known as **Snowy Butte Mill.**   It is still a working mill, and open to the public. Adjacent is a "country store," where stone-ground flour and other products can be purchased.

Butte Falls

This town of 400 or so bills itself as the "biggest little town in Oregon." It is the prototype of the Oregon logging town. Around 1900, a mill was constructed next to the nearby falls, and by 1910 there was a railroad between Butte Falls and Medford. The railroad continued in operation until 1960, when the coming of log trucks made it obsolete.

The old mill by the falls on Big Butte Creek is gone, but the falls are there. It is a delightful spot for a visit. To get to Butte Falls, go north from Medford on OR 62 for 14 miles to Butte Falls Road and turn right for 15 miles. The road to the falls (about 1 mile) is on the left, just before entering town. The falls are not high, perhaps eight feet or so, but the ledge that produces the falls extends across the entire creek, so the total effect is impressive. Near the viewing platform are some concrete foundations belonging to the old mill.

Figure 48 - Butte Creek Mill

Dogs for the Deaf, Inc.

Dogs for the Deaf, located on Wheeler Road near Table Rocks, is a non-profit agency, supported by private funds. Its purpose is to rescue dogs from adoption shelters, and professionally train them to assist deaf or hard of hearing people. These are called "Hearing Dogs," and are trained to be alert to the following sounds: fire/smoke alarm, telephone, door knock, doorbell, oven timer, alarm clock, name call, and baby cry. In addition, they are also obedience trained and socialized. Some dogs, referred to as "Special Needs Dogs," are especially trained to become companions to people with illnesses such as trauma, strokes, chronic illness, and depression.

The dogs chosen are primarily between the ages of eight months and three years old, and are selected for being energetic, friendly, and intelligent. Only about one out of four dogs actually makes it as a "Hearing Dog." The others are adopted as pets, by people who apply for them. In the 27 years of its existence, Dogs for the Deaf has rescued and placed over 2500 dogs.

Funds for Dogs for the Deaf come from individual contributions, service clubs, businesses, foundations, and bequests. Tours are given throughout the year, except on Saturdays, Sundays, and holidays.

Figure 50 - Grants Pass National Historic District

10 Grants Pass
"It's the Climate"

Grants Pass is a delightful city, with a long history. A part of one of the downtown streets has been designated as a National Historic District, with charming buildings, maintained in their historic state. But Grants Pass is also a modern, bustling city with many shopping centers and restaurants. And it is a major destination for tourists, because the city is closely identified with the Rogue River, which runs right through the heart of the city. And it has a terrific climate, along with the rest of the Rogue Valley. A sign that arches across the main street declares, "It's the Climate."

The **Grower's Market,** which is claimed to be the largest open air agricultural market in Oregon, operates each Saturday morning from mid-March to mid-November, behind the Post

Figure 49 - OPPOSITE PAGE - "It's the Climate"

Office on F and 4th Streets. It began in 1986, and features fresh fruits and vegetables, as well as gourmet specialty foods, artists, and crafters.

The **Grants Pass Museum of Art** is located in the National Historic District, and is free of charge. It features collections including sculpture, paintings, and textiles, and has a monthly show of art collections from around the United States. Periodically, it has shows that highlight Oregon or local artists.

Starting in 2003, the Evergreen Federal Bank sponsored the **Bearfest.** The event celebrated the area's black bear population, and consisted of life-sized fiberglass statues of bears, decorated by local artists, that were displayed on the downtown streets of Grants Pass during the summer months. In 2006, the bank sponsored **"An Old Fashioned Celebration of America,"** featuring 23 life-sized replicas of bald eagles, some of them mounted on boulders so pedestrians can look them in the eye.

Grants Pass sponsors many other events and festivals, including a **Spring Wine Stroll** (May), **Antique and Collectible Street Fair** (May), **Wild Rogue Balloon Festival** (June), **Back to the 50s Car Show** (summer), **Art Along the Rogue** (October, featuring chalk street paintings), and **First Friday Art Night** (first Friday night of each month except January).

A major employer in Grants Pass is **Fire Mountain Gems and Beads**. The company began in the 1970s in Southern California, with Native American jewelry. It relocated to Cave Junction in 1986, and then to Grants Pass. The name "Fire Mountain" was chosen because of the heat and pressure processes through which gemstones are created. Today it employs 500 people, and offers a list of over 72,500 jewelry-making items to customers on a wholesale basis.

The city was named for General Ulysses S. Grant, but there is no evidence that General Grant ever visited there. At the time the city was named, Grant had just won the battle of Vicksburg, in the Civil War, and was a national hero. The story is that a road crew working on the road just north of present-day Grants Pass decided to call the low pass at that point (Merlin Hill) Grant's Pass, in his honor, and a stage station nearby was given that name. When the railroad came through, the railroad station was established in its present location in the middle of the city, and the local postmaster wanted to call the Post Office by the name of "Grant." But the postal service said there was already a post office by that name in Oregon, so the name Grant's Pass was chosen, transferring it from the nearby stage station. (The apostrophe was later dropped, because it is the policy of the U.S. Board of Geographical Names not to use apostrophes, unless it is a necessary part of the name, as in O'Brien.)

In Grants Pass, the term "Three Rivers" appears in names such as **Three Rivers Community Hospital,** and the **Three Rivers School District**. I was able to guess what the three rivers were, but thought I should verify my guess by asking some Grants Pass folks who I thought would know the answer. I was surprised at the responses. Most were not sure, and one even included the Klamath as one of the rivers. But the Three Rivers Community Hospital said the rivers are the Rogue, the Illinois, and the Applegate. In fact, at the hospital, the first floor is called "The Rogue," the second floor is "The Illinois," and the third is "The Applegate."

In 2004, a book called "Boomtown USA" included Grants Pass among its top 100 small cities in the country. The criteria included such things as health care, education, recreation, culture, "can-do" atmosphere, leveraging resources, and the like. Especially, Grants Pass was commended for playing up its natural resources.

In 2006, *Mother Earth News* included Grants Pass on its list of "12 Great Places You've Never Heard Of." *Mother Earth News* said that "Southwestern Oregon is a great place to live, with amazing scenery, a mild climate, recreational opportunities at every turn and a high level of support for sustainability." *Mother Earth News* added that Ashland and Medford also were wonderful places, but commented that Grants Pass is more afford-able, while offering many of the same benefits. Of the "12 Great Places", seven were east of the Rocky Mountains, and one was in Alaska (Sitka). The ones in the West, besides Grants Pass, were Grand Junction, Colorado, St. George, Utah, and LaGrande, Oregon.

The Caveman

As you enter Grants Pass from the north, the statue of The Cave-man, almost 20 feet tall, is there to greet you, next to the visitor center. **The Oregon Cavemen**, a booster group composed of local business-men, organized themselves in 1922, to publicize Grants Pass and Josephine County, and to spread good will. They took their name, of course, from the Oregon Caves in near Cave Junction. (See Page 96.) The members, dressed in ani-mal skins, and carrying clubs,

Figure 51 - The Caveman

marched in parades, usually with a rustic cage, in which they would imprison their "victims" chosen from the spectators, preferably an important visitor. But, by the 21st century, the mem-bership had dropped from its high point of 300 members to about 20.

In 2004, someone tried to set the fiberglass caveman statue on fire using a road flare. The members of the Oregon Cavemen stepped forward to have it repaired, and the following year the statue was back in place. Even though the term "cavemen" may have become controver-sial with some, there are many who defend it. The local high school athletic teams are called the "Cavemen," the bridge across the Rogue River at 6th Avenue is called "The Caveman Bridge," and there are many businesses in the Grants Pass area that have the word "Caveman" in their names.

Rogue Community College

Rogue Community College (RCC) was established in 1970, and began operations on an 84-acre wooded campus 5 miles west of Grants Pass, called the **Redwood Campus**. Origi-nally, the focus was on Josephine County. In 1997 the college expanded to include Jackson

Figure 52 - On the Redwood Campus of Rogue Valley Community College

County, and an eight-building complex was developed in downtown Medford, called the **Riverside Campus.** In 2005, the **Table Rock Campus** was established in White City, to offer programs in diesel technology, fire science, construction technology, manufacturing, electronics technology, emergency medical technician, and apprenticeships. As of 2006, RCC had 14,591 students (4,088 full-time equivalent), 100 full-time faculty, and 620 part-time faculty.

RCC offers academic and professional technical programs, courses for college transfer, and continuing education. The professional programs lead to technical certificates or to an Associate of Applied Science degree. Those completing transfer degrees are assured of junior-level standing at any public institution in the Oregon University System.

Special transfer agreements have been made with **Southern Oregon University**, in Ashland, for programs in Early Childhood Education, Criminal Justice, Computer Science, Business, and Human Services. Also, transfer agreements have been made with **Oregon Institute of Technology,** in Klamath Falls, regarding programs in Manufacturing Engineering Technology, Respiratory Care, and pre-professional programs in Dental Hygiene, Medical Imaging Technology, and Geomatics. (Geomatics has to do with surveying and geographical information.) In addition, transfer agreements have been made with **University of Phoenix** for programs in Computer Support, Digital Graphics Design, and Networking. (University of Phoenix, based in Phoenix, Arizona, specializes in online learning through the Internet.)

The **Wiseman Gallery** is located on the Redwood Campus of RCC, with exhibits of local artists and of national artists of emerging importance. The exhibits change regularly.

Riverside Park

Riverside Park, with its lawns, trees, playground, and picnic areas, is highly visible as you cross the Caveman Bridge from the north. It seems like a cool refuge, beside the Rogue River. On Tuesday evenings in the summer, the Chamber of Commerce presents free **Concerts in the Park**, with music ranging from jazz to classical.

Riverside Park is also the principal scene for **Boatnik**, which is held every Memorial Day weekend. Things start on Thursday evening in Riverside Park, with a carnival. The next day is a parade, which passes through downtown Grants Pass and ends in the park, followed by three days of activities including volleyball, arts and crafts, and food booths. The main event, a hydroplane boat race, comes on Monday. The boats start at Riverside Park and race down almost to Galice, and then return to the finish at Riverside Park.

Figure 53 - Riverside Park in Grants Pass

Rogue Theatre and Rogue Music Theatre

These two organizations with similar-sounding names are not connected. The **Rogue Theatre**, located on H Street in downtown Grants Pass, originally was a movie theater, constructed in 1938. In the 1990s, it underwent a renaissance, and became a performing arts center. In 2005, it was listed on the National Register of Historic Places. It's interesting to note that there are at least two other organizations in the U.S. bearing the name "Rogue Theatre" or "Rogue Theatre Company" -- one based in Chicago and the other in Tucson.

The **Rogue Music Theatre** has been offering summer musicals since 1982. It is a non-profit organization that offers its productions in the outdoor ampitheatre at Rogue Community College, and also at Jacksonville's Britt Festival and at Medford's Craterian Ginger Rogers Theater.

Josephine County Fairgrounds

The fair is held in mid-August, and is billed as an "old-fashioned county fair." It includes baking, crafts, and hobby contests, livestock shows, entertainment, square-dancing, carnival rides, pig races, and 4x4 truck pulls.

Horse-racing is held annually at the adjacent **Grants Pass Downs,** on weekends from the middle of May to early July.

NEARBY AREAS

Merlin

Only two other towns in Oregon that I know of are named after birds: Eagle Point and Eagle Creek. (The town of Crow, Oregon, is named after an early settler named James Crow, not the bird.) But the town of **Merlin** is named after a small falcon that once was called "Pigeon Hawk," presumably because it preyed on pigeons. "McAllister" was the original name for the community when it was established in 1885, but it became "Merlin" in 1891. The name reportedly was suggested by a railroad employee, because of the merlins he had observed in the area.

Because the town is located on the main road leading from Grants Pass to the Lower Rogue, and is the staging point for some of the river trips, it calls itself **"The Gateway to the Wild and Scenic Rogue River."** It sponsors a community parade on the first Saturday of each May, and an antique tractor show on Father's Day.

A creek near Merlin, with the intriguing name of **Jump-off Joe Creek**, was apparently named for an incident that occurred in 1828. Joe McLoughlin, son of Dr. John McLoughlin (see page 10) was in a trapping party led by Alexander McLeod. The trappers were camped on this stream one night, and McLoughlin, who came in after dark, fell off a steep bluff and sustained serious injuries.

Wildlife Images

Wildlife Images Rehabilitation and Education Center is a non-profit corporation founded to care for sick, injured, or orphaned wildlife, and to offer educational programs. The great majority of animals treated at the facility are released back into the wild. If it is judged that the animals are unable to live in the wild, they are made a part of the center's educational programs, if possible. Animals treated at the center range from baby squirrels, to bobcats, bears, and bald eagles. The facility is on 24 acres of land next to the Rogue River, about 11 miles from Grants Pass.

Wildlife Images is open year round, except for certain holidays. Visitors are not permitted to walk around the facility without a guide. A volunteer guide will be provided for your tour, but it is necessary to phone in advance, to make arrangements. Call (541) 476-0222. There is no charge for a tour, but donations are encouraged. To get there, take I-5 north to Exit 61, go through Merlin, about 4 miles to Robertson Bridge Road and turn left. Go to second stop sign and turn left on Artlin, go to the stop sign and turn left on Lower River Road. Wildlife Images is the first driveway on the right.

Who was Indian Mary?

While traveling on the road from Merlin to Galice, just beyond Hellgate Canyon, you pass a delightful county park, called **Indian Mary Park.** A historical marker says it is the "Smallest Indian reservation ever created, granted to Indian Mary by the U.S. Government in 1894 in recognition of gratitude to her father, Umpqua Joe, who gave the alarm which saved white settlers in this area from a planned massacre."

Umpqua Joe (sometimes written as Joe Umpqua) and his wife lived with a small band of Indians along the banks of upper Grave Creek, which flows into the Rogue River downstream from the present Indian Mary Park. They were related to the Umpqua tribe, but held themselves to be independent either of the Umpquas or the Rogues. They chose to ally themselves with the white miners in the area, and, at the beginning of the Indian wars in 1852 brought the warning of an impending attack. The miners were able to fortify themselves and fought off the attack in what is called the Battle of Skull Bar. Subsequently, when other Indians in the area were removed to a reservation in the north, the miners asked that Umpqua Joe and his wife be allowed to remain.

Umpqua Joe took up a piece of flat land next to the Rogue River, upstream from where the Battle of Skull Bar was fought. It was there that Mary was born and grew up. Joe occasionally carried miners across the river in his boat, and then constructed a raft-like ferry, in order to make it a regular business.

In 1885, Mary got married. A year later, her father and her husband killed each other in a shoot-out, following an argument. After the double shooting, Mary and her sister remained at the "ranch" on the river, and operated the ferry. At about the same time, Mary filed a homestead application for the land on which she was living.

In 1889, Mary got married for a second time, to Jackson Peters, but the marriage lasted for only a few years. Mary continued to operate the ferry, but it became hard to make a living, and in 1894 she leased her land to a neighbor. She moved with her children to Grants Pass, and supported herself by taking in laundry.

In the same year, the U.S. Government, presumably acting on Mary's homestead application, issued a declaration that it ". . .will hold the land described, for the period of twenty-five years, in trust, for the sole use and benefit of the said Mary Peters." Later, Mary moved to Salem, where her children were then living, and died there in 1921. In 1958, Josephine County bought the land where Mary lived, and created the lovely Indian Mary Park we know today.

Wolf Creek Inn

Modern visitors can be a bit confused by the name of this establishment, because the signs on the freeway say "Wolf Creek Inn," but the archways leading to the inn say "Wolf Creek Tavern." The explanation is that the inn, at an earlier time, apparently was called by the name "Wolf Creek Tavern," in the sense that the term "tavern" was used at that time for a hotel that also sold food. Today, the term "tavern" is generally understood to mean a place that serves alcoholic beverages, so the modern name is "Wolf Creek Inn." When the inn was listed in 1972 on the **National Register of Historic Places,** it was listed under its historic name of "Wolf Creek Tavern."

The inn was constructed in 1883, at about the time the railroad was coming through, and the stagecoach lines were nearing their end. However, it did serve stagecoach travelers during

Figure 54 - Wolf Creek Inn (Wolf Creek Tavern)

the time when stages were still running between Roseburg and Redding, California, prior to the completion of the railroad in 1887.

The inn has been in continuous use since its beginnings, and is the oldest continuously operated hotel in the Pacific Northwest. Among the celebrities who have stayed there are Mary Pickford, Douglas Fairbanks, Jack London, Clark Cable, Carol Lombard, and Orson Welles. It was purchased by the State of Oregon in 1975, and four years were spent in restoring it. It is operated by the Oregon Parks and Recreation Department, with a restaurant and nine guest rooms. It sponsors events such as the **Annual Blues and Microbrew Festival** on Father's Day, and the annual **Oktoberfest** in late September.

Golden Historical District

The Gin Lin Trail in the Applegate Valley provides one example of aggressive hydraulic mining in our area. The mined area near the old ghost town of **Golden** provides another. From I-5, at Exit 76, near Wolf Creek, turn east on Coyote Creek Road and go 3.5 miles to the ghost town. There are a few old buildings, such as the church (1892), a general store (1904), and part of an old residence (1892). Gold was first discovered in the 1850s in the creek below where the town sits, and was mined with the use of sluices until the late 1870s, when high-pressure hydraulic mining was introduced. Mining continued into the mid 20th century. At its height, the town was so active that the stage company made a detour to it from its main line near Wolf Creek.

The area is open to the public, and previously was owned by Golden Coyote Wetlands, Inc., a non-profit organization whose purpose was to maintain the old buildings, and to restore the old mined areas for wildlife habitat. In 2002, the Historic District was added to the National Register of Historic Places. In 2006, the district was purchased by the Oregon Parks and Recreation Department for preservation.

Kerby

Kerbyville (or Kerbeyville, or Kirbyville), about two miles north of Cave Junction, was organized in 1855, and named for the area's first settler, James Kerby (or Kerbey). In 1856, Josephine County was separated from Jackson County, and Kerby was selected as the county seat, a role it lost 30 years later to Grants Pass.

Figure 55 - Golden Community Church

Also in 1856, its name was changed to "Napoleon" by an act of the legislature, perhaps because of the association of the name of the county with the Empress Josephine. However, the name was never popular, and soon was dropped in favor of Kerbyville, and then just Kerby.

Cave Junction

Cave Junction bills itself as the "Home of the Oregon Caves." Some boosters also say it is the "banana belt" of Oregon, in reference to its mild climate, but that title is also claimed by Brookings, on the Southern Oregon coast. It has about 1400 residents, and is the commercial center for the Illinois River Valley. The **Wild Blackberry Arts and Crafts Festival** is held each year in mid-August, and features arts and crafts, food and "great music."

Siskiyou Field Institute

The Institute offers a remarkable variety of natural history courses, focusing on the Klamath-Siskiyou region. Courses range from one to six days in length, and include topics such as ecology, birds, botany, photography, astronomy, climate, fish, ethnobiology, and river guiding. Programs culminating in the award of a Naturalist Certificate are available. Some of the courses carry college credit, either at Southern Oregon University or Humboldt State University in Arcata, California.

In 2006, Siskiyou Field Institute (SFI) and Southern Oregon University joined as partners to purchase the 870-acre Deer Creek Ranch near Selma, Oregon. The ranch has been named the **Deer Creek Center for Field Research and Education.** It will serve as a headquarters for SFI, and provide year-round facilities for education and research.

Oregon Caves

When the **Oregon Caves** first came to public attention in the 1870s, they were widely billed by newspapers as "a worthy rival to Mammoth Caves in Kentucky," although they are not nearly as extensive as Mammoth Caves. Nevertheless, they are charming, and are decorated with the calcite formations that one expects to see in caves. Tens of thousands of people visit them every year, and in the middle of summer there can be long waits to get in. The round trip is approximately one mile, with about 500 steps involved. It is not for people in poor condition, or for small children. Also, visitors are warned about bumping their heads on rock outcroppings.

In the canyon next to the caves a small village was constructed, consisting principally of two historic buildings, the **Chalet** and the **Chateau**. The canyon is so narrow and constricted that parking has been provided about 900 feet back down the road, and most visitors walk the last 900 feet to get to the caverns.

The Chalet, which serves as the visitor center, was constructed in 1923 (rebuilt in 1941), and the six-story Chateau, which has rental rooms and a restaurant, was finished in 1934. The Chateau is tucked into the canyon in such a way that it appears to be only two stories high from the front, but is six stories high when viewed from the canyon below.

The creek flowing from the caves plunges directly into a pool in front of the Chateau. Both the Chalet and Chateau came close to being destroyed in the "Christmas Flood" of 1964. Much of Oregon experienced destruction from floods at that time.

The caves lie 19 miles east of Cave Junction, via OR 46. **Grayback Campground,** maintained by the U.S. Forest Service, is 11.4 miles from Cave Junction on OR 46, and is a delightful spot. A wheelchair-accessible trail, called the **Grayback Interpretive Trail,** has been constructed along Sucker Creek, next to the day-use area in the campground. Sucker Creek allegedly got its name because some of the early inhabitants of the area were from Illinois, and named the creek for their state, which had the nickname of the "Sucker State". This name was given, according to one story, because some early settlers of Illinois had been "suckered" into buying substandard land by eastern speculators. However, the official web site for the State of Illinois does not mention this nickname, but says that the state's nickname is the "Prairie State."

Figure 56 - The Chateau and the Chalet, at Oregon Caves

Rough and Ready Botanical Wayside.

The wayside is 5 miles south of Cave Junction on US 199, next to Rough and Ready Creek. The creek got its name from miners in the area, to honor President Zachary Taylor, who was called "Old Rough and Ready." There is a small parking area, and a trail leads through the area. The surroundings are rather scraggy-looking, and one might wonder why it merits a name like "botanical wayside." But the underlying geological structure consists of a rock called serpentine. Most plants don't grow well in serpentine soils (which accounts for the scraggy appearance), but there are other plants that thrive in serpentine, and some that won't grow anywhere else. Thus, serpentine areas, like this one, are of great botanical interest.

11 A Multitude of Parks

The Rogue Valley has an amazing array of parks, as befits its location, surrounded by beautiful mountains and forests. Many of the major parks and campgrounds are listed below. City parks are not included. Each park is shown by number on the maps in this section.

Bear Creek Greenway

(1) The **Bear Creek Greenway** is an unusual park -- 20 miles long, when it is complete, and only a few feet wide. (At this writing, the section near Barnett Road, in south Medford, was awaiting the completion of a major freeway interchange.) The trail is paved, and is suitable for joggers, walkers, bicyclists, and wheelchairs. Mostly, it is lined with trees, with Bear Creek near by. In the built-up area of downtown Medford the creek is still near by, but in places the trail actually is under the freeway.

The Greenway can be accessed from many points. Here are four:

South terminus (Ashland): From Oak and Nevada streets, go one block west on Nevada Street to Helman Street, and turn right on the narrow paved road.

Lynn Newbry Park (Talent): Use Exit 21 from I-5, and go toward Talent. The entrance to Lynn Newbry Park is less than 100 yards from the freeway, on the left.

Bear Creek Park (Medford): Use Exit 27 from I-5, at Barnett Road. Go to Highland Drive, and turn left. There is an entrance to the park on the left, about 0.2 mile along Highland Drive.

North terminus (Central Point): To get to this terminus, use Exit 33 from I-5, and turn east on East Pine Street. Go 0.2 mile to Peninger Road and turn left. Turn right into the large parking area. The trail goes to the right, under the bridge.

North Mountain Park Nature Center

The nature center offers special classes and other programs for adults and children, about the natural history of the area. Nature trails pass through different areas of the park, including next to Bear Creek, offering chances to see birds and other wildlife. Three soccer fields, two softball fields, and two baseball fields are also a part of North Mountain Park. Located on North Mountain Avenue northeast of Nevada Street.

State Parks

(2) **Casey State Recreation Area.** Picnicking, boat ramp, fishing. Northeast of Medford, 29 miles on OR 62.

(3) **Illinois River Forks State Park.** Picnicking, fishing. South of Cave Junction, one mile on US 199.

Figure 57 - OPPOSITE PAGE - Bear Creek Greenway

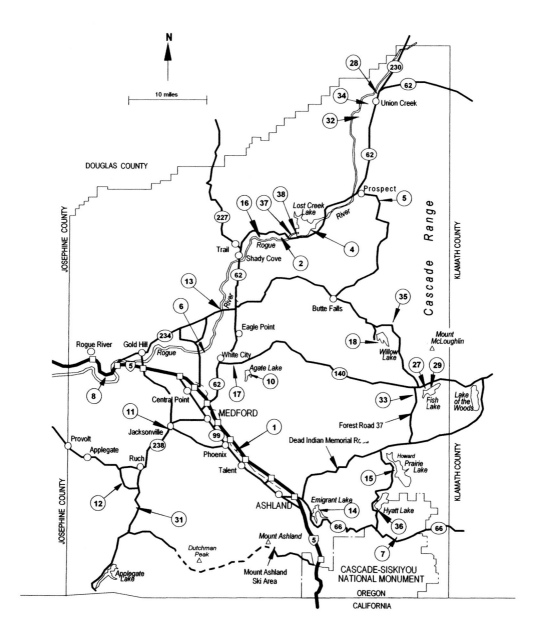

Figure 58- Jackson County

100

(4) Joseph H. Stewart State Recreation Area. Picnicking, camping, RV hookups, marina, boat ramps, playgrounds, hiking and biking trails, fishing, swimming. Northeast of Medford, 35 miles on OR 62.

(5) Prospect State Scenic Viewpoint. Picnicking, hiking trails, waterfalls. Off OR 62, one mile south of Prospect.

(6) Tou Velle State Recreation Site (Tou Velle State Park). Picnicking, boat ramp, trails, swimming. From Medford, go north six miles on OR 62 to Antelope Road, turn west. Go two miles to Table Rock Road and turn right one mile to park.

(7) Tub Springs State Wayside. Historic site, picnicking. East of Ashland, 18 miles on OR 66.

(8) Valley of the Rogue State Park. Picnicking, camping, RV hookups, yurts, boat ramp, nature trail, fishing. Off I-5 at Exit 45B, 12 miles east of Grants Pass.

(9) Wolf Creek Inn State Heritage Site. Historic site, restaurant, rooms, special events. Off I-5 at Exit 76, 20 miles north of Grants Pass.

Jackson County Parks

(10) Agate Lake County Park. Boat ramp, fishing. About three miles east of White City, off OR 140.

(11) Britt Gardens. Picnicking. Two blocks west of downtown Jacksonville.

(12) Cantrall-Buckley County Park. Picnicking, camping. Nine miles west of Jacksonville, off OR 238.

(13) Dodge Bridge. Boat launch, fishing. About one mile west of OR 62, on OR 234.

(14) Emigrant Lake Recreation Area. Picnicking, camping, RV hookups, boating, swimming, 230-foot water slide. Six miles east of Ashland on OR 66.

(15) Howard Prairie Lake Recreation Area. Picnicking; camping at Grizzly Campground, Willow Point Campground, Klum Landing Campground, and Lily Glen Equestrian Facility; boating, sailing, fishing, boat launch. Private resort and campground at Howard Prairie Resort. Seventeen miles east of Ashland, on Dead Indian Memorial Road to Hyatt Prairie Road and turn right.

(16) Rogue Elk County Park. Picnicking, campground, RV hookups, fishing, swimming. Twenty-two miles north of Medford on OR 62.

(17) Sports Park. Softball, drag strip, go-kart track, dirt oval track, shooting range, fishing ponds. Located at OR 140 and Kershaw Road, in White City.

(18) Willow Lake County Park. Picnicking, camping, RV hookups, cabins, boating, fishing, swimming. Eight miles east of Butte Falls.

Josephine County Parks

(19) Almeda Park. Picnicking, camping, yurt, boat ramp, fishing. About 16 miles west of Merlin on Merlin-Galice Road.

(20) Cathedral Hills Trail Network. Hiking, biking, and equestrian trails. About three miles south of Grants Pass on OR 238, to Espey Road. The park is about ½ mile, on Espey Road.

(21) Indian Mary Park. The "showcase" of the Josephine County Park system. Picnicking, camping, hookups, yurts, boat ramp, fishing. About seven miles west of Merlin, on Merlin-Galice Road.

(22) Tom Pearce Park. Picnicking, softball, fishing. Grants Pass, follow Foothill Blvd. to Pierce Park Road, turn right to park.

(23) Lake Selmac. Picnicking, camping, RV hookups, yurts, boat ramp, ball fields, sailing, fishing, swimming. From south of Selmac, go left on Lakeshore Drive about two miles to park.

(24) Schroeder Park. Picnicking, camping, RV hookups, boat ramp, tennis and basketball courts, ballfields. Go west from Grants Pass about one mile on US 199, right on Redwood Avenue about 1½ miles, right on Willow Lane about one mile.

(25) Whitehorse Park. Picnicking, camping, RV hookups, boat ramp, bird sanctuary, playground, fishing. From Grants Pass, go about ½ mile on G Street to Upper River Road, and then about six miles to park.

(26) Wolf Creek Park. Campground, RV hookups. Near historic Wolf Creek Tavern in Wolf Creek.

Campgrounds in Rogue River-Siskiyou National Forest

There are 64 listed campgrounds in the Rogue River-Siskiyou National Forest, some of them with only 1 or 2 sites, and some relatively hard to reach. Only a few of the larger campgrounds, reachable by paved roads, and within Jackson or Josephine Counties, are shown below:

(27) Doe Point. Next to Fish Lake, 30 miles east of Medford on OR 140.

(28) Farewell Bend. On Rogue River, next to OR 62, one mile north of Union Creek.

(29) Fish Lake. Next to Fish Lake, 31 miles east of Medford on OR 140.

(30) Grayback. Next to Sucker Creek, next to OR 46, 11 miles east of Cave Junction.

(31) Jackson. On Applegate River, 10 miles south of Ruch.

(32) Natural Bridge. On Rogue River, near OR 62, one mile south of Union Creek.

(33) North Fork. On North Fork of Little Butte Creek, 28 miles east of Medford on OR 140, and then one mile south on Forest Road 37.

(34) Union Creek. On Rogue River, next to OR 62, adjacent to village of Union Creek.

(35) Whiskey Spring. Ten miles east of Butte Falls.

Cascade-Siskiyou National Monument (BLM)

(36) Hyatt Lake Lake Recreation Complex. Picnicking, two campgrounds (Hyatt Lake Campground and Wildcat Campground), horse camp, two boat ramps, softball, volleyball, basketball, fishing, swimming. Pacific Crest Trail runs near by. At south end of Hyatt Lake. Go 17 miles on OR 66, turn north at Green Springs Inn, and go three miles. A "Watchable Wildlife Site" is on west side of lake.

Corps of Engineers

(37) McGregor Park. Picnicking, nature center, fishing. Turn on Takelma Drive, 29 miles north of Medford, on OR 62.

(38) Rivers Edge Park. Picnicking, fishing, bird watching. This is the location of "Holy Water." (See Page 19.) Off Takelma Drive, 0.2 mile beyond McGregor Park (see above).

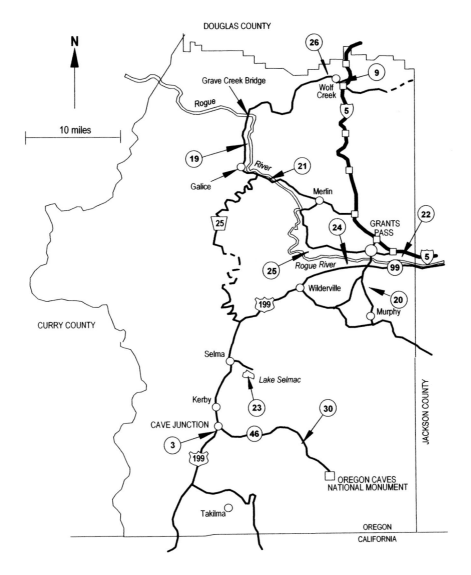

Figure 59 - Josephine County

103

Jackson County Golf Courses

Bear Creek Golf Course and Range. 9 holes. Public. 2355 S. Pacific Hwy., Medford.

Cedar Links Golf Club. 18 holes. Public. 3155 Cedar Links Dr., Medford.

Centennial Golf Club. 18 holes. Public. 1900 N. Phoenix Rd., Medford.

Eagle Point Golf Course. 18 holes. Public. 100 Eagle Point Dr., Eagle Point.

Laurel Hill Golf Course. 9 holes. Public. 9450 Old Stage Rd., Central Point.

Oak Knoll Golf Course. 9 holes. Public. 3070 Hwy 66, Ashland.

Quail Point Golf Course. 9 holes. Public. 1200 Mira Mar Ave., Medford.

Rogue Valley County Club. Both 9-hole and 18-hole courses. Private. 2660 Hillcrest Rd., Medford.

Stewart Meadows. 9 holes. Public. 1301 S. Holly St., Medford.

Stone Ridge Golf Club. 18 holes. Public. 500 E. Antelope, Eagle Point.

Veterans Administration Domiciliary Golf Course. 9 holes. Private. Domiciliary, White City.

Josephine County Golf Courses

Applegate Golf. 9 holes. Public. 7350 New Hope Rd., Grants Pass.

Colonial Valley Golf Course. 9 holes. Public. 75 Nelson Way, Grants Pass.

Dutcher Creek Golf Course. 9 holes. Public. 4611 Upper River Rd., Grants Pass.

Grants Pass Golf Club. 18 holes. Semi-private. 230 Espey Rd., Grants Pass.

Hillebrand's Paradise Ranch Resort. 3 holes. Resort. 7000 Monument Dr., Grants Pass

Illinois Valley Golf Club. 9 holes. Semi-private. Redwood Hwy. and Laurel Rd. Cave Junction.

Red Mountain Golf Course. 9 holes. Public. 324 N Schoolhouse Creek Rd, Grants Pass.

Mount Ashland Ski Area

The Mount Ashland Ski Area has been referred to as being "in the heart of the Southern Oregon Alps." It has four chair lifts, 23 different runs, night skiing, and 100 miles of cross-country trails. From I-5, take the Mt. Ashland Exit (Exit 6), and follow the signs eight miles on the paved high-standard road.

The ski area began in 1963, as an outgrowth of ski classes held by Southern Oregon State College (now Southern Oregon University). The area is owned by the City of Ashland, and is operated by a non-profit corporation called Mt. Ashland Association.

References

(For a reference taken from the Internet, the name, date, and web address are given.)

Adams, Liliana Osses. 2005. *Shakespeare in Ashland, Oregon.*
http://www.zwoje-scrolls.com/zwoje43/text29p.htm

The Applegate Trail. 2006 -- www.webtrail.com/applegate

Applegate's Road to Oregon. 2006.
http://www.endoftheoregontrail.org/road2oregon/sa22applegate.html

Archibold, Randal C. "Off the Beaten Path," *New York Times,* 7-30-06.

Barrett, Carol. 1998. *As it Was -- Stories from the History of Southern Oregon and Northern California.* Jefferson Public Radio, Ashland, OR.

Bastasch, Rick. 1998. *Waters of Oregon.* Oregon State University Press, Corvallis, OR.

Begnoche, Don. 1999. *Siskiyou Sundays -- A Tour of Southwestern Oregon.* Don Begnoche, Ashland, OR.

Bernstein, Art. 2001. *Hiking Oregon's Southern Cascades and Siskiyous.* A Falcon Guide. Globe Pequot Press, Guilford, Conn.

"Best Places to Retire." CNNMoney 2006. http://money.cnn.com/best/bpretire/

Biography of General Philip Kearny. 2006.
http://www.geocities.com/athens/aegean/6732/files/kearny1.html

Booth, Percy T. 1975. *The Legend of Indian Mary and Umpqua Joe.* Josephine County Historical Society, Grants Pass, OR.

Booth, Percy T. 1997. *Until the Last Arrow -- A True Story of the Indian Wars and Gold Rushes that Opened the Last Frontier of Oregon Country -- the Rogue River Valley.* B. and B. Publishing, Coos Bay, OR.

Booth, Percy T. 1970. *Valley of the Rogues.* B. and B. Publishing, Coos Bay, OR.

Live at Britt Festivals -- Britt Concerts Under the Stars. 2005. Britt Festivals, Medford, OR.

Buck Prairie Winter Recreation Area. 2003. Bureau of Land Management, Medford District.

Cascade Range Volcanoes and Volcanics. 2006. U.S. Geological Survey.
http://vulcan.wr.usgs.gov/Volcanoes/Cascades/description_cascade_range.html

Chinese Exclusion Act. 1882. http://www.mtholyoke.edu/acad/intrel/chinex.htm

Cole M. Rivers Hatchery. Oregon Dept. of Fish and Wildlife.

Community Profiles. 2005. Grants Pass/Josephine County Chamber of Commerce, Grants Pass, OR.

Craterian Theatre, Medford, Oregon. 2006.
http://www.pstos.org/instruments/or/medford/craterian.htm

Craterian Performances, 2006-07 Season. Craterian Performances Co., Medford, OR.

Davis, Charles George. *The South Road, and the Route Across Southern Oregon.* 2000. Emigrants West, North Plains, OR.

DeNevi, Don. 1976. *Western Train Robberies.* Celestial Arts, Millbrae, CA.

DiGiovanni, Nicholas. *The Microscopy of Hair.* 2006.
    http://www.nabt.org/sub/pdf/HAIR2.pdf

Dogs for the Deaf, Inc. 2006.   http://www.dogsforthedeaf.org/

Eder, Tamara. *Mammals of Washington and Oregon.* 2002. Lone Pine Publishing, Edmonton, AB, Canada.

Elliott, T.C., ed. 1910. *The Peter Skene Ogden Journals.*
    http://www.xmission.com/~drudy/mtman/html/ogden.html

Elk Populations in Southwestern Oregon. 2005.
    http://www.dfw.state.or.us/news/2005/April/026.asp

Emerson, William. 1996. *The Applegate Trail of 1846.* Ember Enterprises, Ashland, OR.

Euro-American Presence in the Mid-Wlllamette Valley, 1811-1844. 2003.
    http://www.ci.corvallis.or.us/index.php?option=content&task=view&id=106&Itemid=64

"Fewer homes sell, but prices still high," *Mail Tribune,* May 9, 2006, p. 6A.

Foley, Anne. 1994. *On the Greensprings.* Published by the Friends of the Greensprings.

The Fort Lane Archaeology Project: Current Research. 2005. Southern Oregon University, Ashland, OR.   http://www.sou.edu/SOCIOL/arch/Fort%20Lane/Research.html

Gibson, Elizabeth. 2004. *The Rogue River Indian War* (Parts 1 and 2).
    http://www.suite101.com/article.cfm/old_west/108134

Ginger Rogers at AllExperts. 2006.
    http://experts.about.com/e/g/gi/Ginger_Rogers.htm

Ginger Rogers at Reel Classics: Biography. 2006.
    http://www.reelclassics.com/Actresses/Ginger/ginger-bio.htm

Gin Lin Mining Trail. 1997. U.S. Dept. of Agriculture, Forest Service, Medford, OR.

Grants Pass Oregon in Southern Rogue Valley. 2006.
    http://www.southernoregon.com/grantspass/index.html

Great Rivers -- Rogue River. 2006.
    www.flyanglersonline.com/features/greatrivers/rogue/

Grey, Zane. 1929. *Rogue River Feud.* Pocket Books, a division of Simon and Schuster, New York.

Henkle, Joy. 2006. *"Hiking Oregon's Rogue River Trail."*
   http://www.oregon.com/trips/rogueriverhike.cfm

Historic Earthquakes in the Pacific Northwest. 2006. Oregon Department of Geology and Mineral Industries.
   http://www.oregongeology.com/sub/earthquakes/HistoricEQs.htm

The Historic Wolf Creek Inn. 2006. http://www.rogueweb.com/wolfcreekinn/

A History of Chinese Immigration to Oregon. 2002.
   http://everything2.com/index.pl?node_id=880926

The History of Medford, Oregon. 2006.
   http://www.ci.medford.or.us/Page.asp?NavID=78

History of Oregon BLM. 2006. http://www.oregonheritageforests.org/history

The History of Prospect Hotel. 2006. www.prospecthotel.com/history

Jackson County Air Quality Annual Report. 2004-2005. Jackson County Environmental Health, Medford, OR.

Jackson County, Oregon: Information from Answers.com. 2006.
   http://www.answers.com/topic/jackson-county-oregon

Jackson County Oregon Golf Courses. 2006.
   http://www.golfable.com/golfcourses/county/Jackson_County_OR

Jackson County Parks. 2006. http://www.jacksoncountyparks.com/

Jacksonville, Oregon Overview. 2006.
   http://www.nwsource.com/travel/scr/tf_detail.cfm?dt=3948

Jacksonville Woodlands Association. 2006 www.jvwoodlands.org

Jefferson Public Radio. 2006 www3.jeffnet.org

Josephine County Oregon Golf Courses. 2006.
   http://www.golfable.com/golfcourses/county/Josephine_County_OR

Josephine County Parks. 2006.
   http://www.co.josephine.or.us/SectionIndex.asp?SectionID=132

The Klamath Bird Observatory. 2006.   http://www.klamathbird.org/

Kramer, George. 1992. *Camp White -- City in the Agate Desert.* Camp White 50th Anniversary Committee, White City, OR.

Krants, Grover S. 1999. *Bigfoot Sasquatch Evidence.* Hancock House, Blaine, Washington.

List of Mountain Lion Attacks. 2006. http://cougarinfo.com/attacks.htm

Map of Oregon Territory. 1843.
   http://memory.loc.gov/cgi-bin/query/r?ammem/upboverbib:@field(DOCID+@lit(maps39))

McArthur, Lewis A. 1992. *Oregon Geographic Names, Sixth Edition.* Oregon Historical Society Press, Portland, OR.

Medford Oregon Visitors and Conventions Business Site. 2004.
http://visitmedford.mind.net/modules.php?name=Encyclopedia&op=list_content&eid=22

Meier, Gary and Gloria. 1987. *The Knights of the Whip.* Timeline Publishing Co., Bellevue, WA.

Momsen, Joan. 2006. *Grants Pass, Oregon History.*
http://www.webtrail.com/history/grantspass.shtml

Mt. Ashland Ski Area. 2006. http://www.mtashland.com/

Mount McLoughlin Volcano, Oregon. 2006. U.S. Geological Survey.
http://vulcan.wr.usgs.gov/Volcanoes/McLoughlin/description_mcloughlin.html

Mountain Lion Facts. 2000. Oregon Department of Fish and Wildlife, Salem, OR.

National Fish and Wildlife Forensics Laboratory. 2006.
http://www.lab.fws.gov/about.html

National Register of Historic Places. 2006. National Park Service.
http://www.cr.nps.gov/nr/

The Oldtimer -- An Annual Publication of the Josephine County Historical Society. Vol. 32, No. 5, 1998.

Oregon Air Quality Data Summaries. 2005. Department of Environmental Quality, Salem. OR.

Oregon Cabaret Theatre. 2006. http://www.oregoncabaret.com/history.html

Oregon DEQ: Frequently Asked Quetions. 2006.
http://www.deq.state.or.us/about/faq.htm

Oregon Employment Department. Fall, 2005. *Regional Profile, Industry Employment in Region 8.*

Oregon History: Dead Indian Memorial Road. 2006.
http://www.oregon.com/history/hm/dead_indian_memorial.cfm

Oregon Parks and Recreation Department: State Parks. 2006.
http://www.oregon.gov/OPRD/PARKS/

Oregon Parks Association - Josephine County. 2006.
http://www.orparks.org/a_oregonparks/josephine.htm

Oregon Shakespeare Festival. 2006. Ashland, OR.

Pacificorp. 2006. http://www.pacificorp.com/

Peter Britt: The Man Beyond the Camera 2006 www.peterbritt.org

Ramsey, Roger. 2006. *Golden, Oregon History.*
   http://www.webtrail.com/history/golden.shtml

RealEstate.com 2006. http://www.realestate.com/

Reyes, Chris. 1994. *The Table Rocks of Jackson County: Islands in the Sky.* Last Minute Publications, Ashland, OR.

Roads of Crater Lake National Park. 2002. www.nps.gov/crla/hrs/hrs8.htm

Rogue Community College. 2006. www.roguecc.edu

Rogue River Ranch National Historic Site. 2000. Bureau of Land Management, Medford, OR.

Rogue River-Siskiyou National Forest -- Welcome! 2006.
   http://www.fs.fed.us/r6/rogue-siskiyou/

The Rogue Theatre. 2006. http://www.roguetheatre.com/

Rogue Valley Cup Soccer Tournament. 2006.
   http://www.rvcupsoccer.com/home.htm

Rogue Valley Growers and Crafters Market. 2006.
   http://www.ashlandchamber.com/DirectoryDetails.asp?MemberID=1324

Sauls, Jane. 2004. "Southern Oregon Bigfoot Lore," *Jacksonville Oregon News,* Bigfoot Field Researchers Organization, Media Article #411.
   http://www.bfro.net/GDB/show_article.asp?id=411

ScienceWorks Hands-on Museum. 2006. http://www.scienceworksmuseum.org/

Siskiyou Trail. 2006. http://en.wikipedia.org/wiki/Siskiyou_Trail

The Siskiyou Trail: The Archaeology of an Emigrant Wagon Road. 2002.
   http://www.sou.edu/SOCIOL/arch/SISKIYOU.HTM

Southern Oregon University. 2006 -- www.worldclimate.com

Southern Oregon University Extended Campus. 2006.
   http://www.sou.edu/ecp/mfd/

Southworth, Darlene. 2006. *Whetstone Savannah.*
   http://www.sou.edu/BIOLOGY/Faculty/Southworth/site.htm

SOU Graduate Studies. 2006. http://www.sou.edu/GraduateStudies/

"The State of Jefferson secession movement of 1941." 2006 --
   http://sisnet.ssku.k12.ca.us/~msusdftp/jones/ian/historypg1.html

Talent Irrigation District, District History 2006. www.talentid.org/

Theater History and the Ginger Rogers Connection. 2004.
www.craterian.org/historyginger2b.html

Trail, Pepper. Recognizing Paradise: The World Discovers the Klamath- Siskiyou Ecoregion", *The Jefferson Monthly Magazine,* Vol. 22, no. 2, February 1998.

Union Creek Resort. 2006. www.unioncreekoregon.com

U.S. Census Bureau. 2006. *State & County QuickFacts.* --
http://quickfacts.census.gov

U.S. Geological Survey. 2005. *Geographic Names Information System.*
http://geonames.usgs.gov/otherlinks.html

Vaughan, M. R., and Pelton, M. R. *Black Bears in North America.* 2005.
http://biology.usgs.gov/s+t/noframe/c286.htm

Webber, Bert and Margie. 1994. *Jacksonville Oregon - Antique Town in a Modern Age.* Webb Research Group, Medford, OR.

Webber, Bert and Margie. 1996. *The Lure of Medford -- An Oregon Documentary.* Webb Research Group, Medford, OR.

Webber, Bert and Margie. 1988. *Oregon's Great Train Holdup.* Webb Research Group, Medford, OR.

Webber, Bert and Margie. 1997. *The Siskiyou Line - Adventures in Railroading.* Webb Research Group, Medford, OR.

Welcome to Jacksonville, Oregon. 2006. http://www.el.com/to/jacksonville/

Wells, Gail. "Scientists, managers outline black-tailed deer decline." January 21, 2005. Oregon State University News and Communication Services, Corvallis, OR.

Wildlife Images Rehabilitation and Education Center. 2006. www.wildlifeimages.org

Williams, Bill. 1998. *Where the Trails Are (5th ed.)* Independent Printing Co., Ashland, OR.

Wines Northwest. 2006 -- www.winesnw.com

Wolf Creek Inn. 2006 Oregon Parks and Recreation Department.
http://www.thewolfcreekinn.com/
http://www.oregonstateparks.org/park_108.php

The World Almanac and Book of Facts. 2002. World Almanac Books, New York, NY.

World Climate: Weather - rainfall and temperature data. 2006 --
www.worldclimate.com

"You can search for Bigfoot near Applegate". September 19, 2005. *The Mail Tribune,* Medford, Oregon.

INDEX

INDEX